WOMEN WITH AIDS AND THEIR CHILDREN

D0103141

SHARON E. WALKER

GARLAND PUBLISHING, INC.
A MEMBER OF THE TAYLOR & FRANCIS GROUP
NEW YORK & LONDON / 1998

Library of Congress Cataloging-in-Publication Data

Walker, Sharon E., 1949–
  Women with AIDS and their children / Sharon E. Walker.
      p.   cm. — (Children of poverty)
  Includes bibliographical references and index.
  ISBN 0-8153-3008-1 (alk. paper)
    1. AIDS (Disease)—Social aspects—United States. 2. AIDS
(Disease)—United States—Psychological aspects. 3. Women—
Diseases—Social aspects—United States. 4. Women—Diseases—
United States—Psychological aspects. 5. AIDS (Disease) in chil-
dren—United States. I. Title. II. Series.
  RA644.A25W33 1997
  362.1'969792'008209073—dc21
                                                          97-31032

Printed on acid-free, 250-year-life paper
Manufactured in the United States of America

This book is dedicated:

To the thirteen courageous women who shared their time, energy and passion so that other women and children with HIV/AIDS could be better understood and supported in their valiant struggle.

With love and appreciation to my best friend, Mick Walker, whose constant support and unfaltering faith have facilitated the navigation of my work. It would not be possible to explain all that he has done or the meaning it has had for me.

and

To Meagan and Kara

Contents

List of Tables

Preface

This book is about courageous women with AIDS who revealed their emotional pain and the concomitant struggles of living with HIV+, and their children. They describe their psychological reactions to the diagnosis itself and to the disease trajectory, and the way in which living with HIV has impacted their relationships with their children. Most of the women either had children with pediatric AIDS, were uncertain of their child's diagnosis at the time of the research, or had experienced the death of a child through vertical transmission. They eloquently describe their valiant attempts at caring for their children while coping with their own disease process. Although some of the participants had supportive families who were aware of their disease, some feared disclosure and thereby were prevented from obtaining the support that they so intensely needed.

In the last several years and in the time since the research for this book was conducted, new treatment for AIDS has been introduced that could change the possible course of the AIDS virus and therefore, the life span of trajectory of those living with it. The drugs, called protease inhibitors, appear to completely suppress the AIDS virus. These drugs block one step in the reproduction cycle of HIV and appear to slow its progression. When protease inhibitors are combined with other older drugs used to treat AIDS, the virus appears to stop reproducing. Although the use of these drugs represent a welcome and hopeful advance in the treatment of HIV+/AIDS, they do not represent a cure. HIV+/AIDS continues to be the leading cause of death among people ages 25-44 and continues to be a leading cause of death in women and children. The drugs themselves are very costly and not universally available, involve strict adherence to medication regimes, and are not similarly effective in all people.

As the treatment possibilities for people with AIDS continues to develop, the numbers of women with AIDS continue to increase dramatically. Although these treatments could prolong the lives of women with AIDS, the treatments to not address the fundamental issues that most of these women confront on a daily basis. Most women with AIDS live in urban areas where poverty and crime are daily facts of life. If they cannot conceal the reality of their diagnosis, they routinely face stigma and disenfranchisement related to the virus itself and to the presumed methods of transmission. As reported, they constantly grapple with virus-related fear of disease progression and anxiety related to society's view of their culpability and contagion. If they reveal that they have HIV+, they are concerned about being seen as "dirty," and about being shunned as a result. The societal stigma associated with AIDS has not been changed by any of the medical advances. The difficulties that women with AIDS incur as they navigate through their own disease process and that of their children who are similarly infected continue. Although the good news is that the medical advances can prolong lives, the bad news is that programs and services have not expanded to cope with increased needs as women and children live longer with the virus. Mothers with AIDS continue to contend with their own disease process and possibly that of their child. They continue to be confronted with the psychological sequelae that are associated with chronic and possibly terminal illness while they face similar issues with their seropositive children and/or as they depend on their healthy children for psychological and physical support. Although programs and services do exist that attempt to meet the needs of women and children, their content and availability need to be expanded in order to provide women with AIDS the care that they and their children need. It is essential that we address the psycho-social needs of women and children with AIDS in order to improve the quality of their lives and in order to prevent children without the virus from caring for family members for prolonged periods of time.

Health care providers who have preconceived views of women with AIDS as being uncaring and neglectful will find their comments to be elucidating. Although the women interviewed reported that they consistently cared for their children at their own expense, they also indicated that virus-related symptoms and stressors precluded them from providing the optimal care that they so wanted to sustain. It is essential to heed the words of the women as they describe the anguish that they feel, the difficulties that they face, and the lengths that they go to to care for their children. It is essential to pay attention to their "cries for help" as they describe the burden of living with chronic illness that is frequently concealed from potential sources of help. The voices of these women are telling us what is needed in terms of care and support and also provide implications for prevention.

Since the research was conducted, I have been contacted by several families of participants who have died. They emphasized the need to disseminate and elucidate the eloquent words of these women and described their fervent hope that the research findings and recommendations would accurately portray their situations and the changes that were needed. One woman requested that the book be read to her as she lay dying. She was concerned that mothers with AIDS were seen as not caring and/or were seen as neglectful of their children. In another instance, the mother of a twenty-year-old woman who had died as a result of AIDS contacted me to relay the significance that participation in the research had had for her daughter. She had located information about the study in her safeguarded belongings after she died. It was her daughter's hope that publication of the material would aid in prevention; it was the mother's hope that she could develop meaning in her daughter's death with the hope that people will read the book and listen to the voices of the women who describe their relationships, their grief and their hope.

It is my hope that those who read this book will be spurred to understanding and action by the courageous lives and deaths of the women described.

Acknowledgments

It is essential that I begin by thanking the women who allowed their stories to be told throughout this book. Their courage and love in the face of extreme adversity were inspirational to me.

I would like to thank the many people who supported this project and whose suggestions were crucial. The initial idea for the research was suggested by William Halikias, Psy.D. Suggestions and feedback were generously contributed by Dusty Miller, Ed.D., Barbara Belcher-Timme, Psy.D. and Lorraine Mangione, Ph.D.

The directors, physicians, nurses, case managers, and social workers affiliated with the programs that assisted me in locating participants go unnamed, in order to protect confidentiality, but have my utmost thanks.

My editors, Tania Bissell and Chuck Bartelt, at Garland Publishing, Inc. were most helpful when technical problems seemed insurmountable.

Two women have profoundly impacted my work in psychology. Kathleen Bollerud, Ed.D. has shared her clinical expertise and has provided numerous learning opportunities, as well as unparalleled support and encouragement. I am extremely appreciative of all that she has contributed to my professional growth. The work of Therese Rando, Ph.D. has been formative in the development of my interest and competence in the field of trauma and complicated mourning.

Finally, I would like to thank my family, Mick, Meagan and Kara, for their humor, patience, and encouragement throughout this process. Without their understanding, this book would not have been possible.

Women with AIDS
and Their Children

I

Introduction

PROBLEM

Women comprise the fastest growing population of PWA (People with AIDS, a commonly used term in the literature) with the number of reported cases among women increasing by 37 percent in 1991 (Andrews, Williams & Neil, 1993; Krieger & Margo, 1994). According to the Centers for Disease Control (1996), women represent twenty percent of the adults/adolescents with AIDS; AIDS is now the fourth-leading cause of death among women between 25 and 44. Women with HIV+ or AIDS are typically non-White (approximately 75% of the women are African or Latina), economically disadvantaged, and disenfranchised from the health care delivery system (Andrews et al., 1993; Antoni et al., 1992; Krieger & Margo, 1994; Levine & Dubler, 1990; Stuber, 1992; Ybarra, 1991). Antoni et al. report that women with HIV+ progress in disease three times faster than sociodemographically similar men and that the survival time for women is half that of men. Kalichman (1995) reports that women with HIV+/AIDS experience greater prejudice and disenfranchisement than men who have sexually contracted HIV infection.

Vertical transmission, or infection that is thought to be passed from the mother to the infant (Canosa, 1991; Carovano, 1994; Coleman, 1991; James, 1988; Septimus, 1990; Stuber, 1992; Wiener, Theut, Steinberg, Riekert, & Pizzo, 1994), accounts for the majority of cases of pediatric AIDS. Stuber asserts that pediatric AIDS will become one of the leading causes of childhood death in any age group within the next decade. Pediatric AIDS is currently among the the leading causes of death in children older than one year (Kalichman, 1995). The diagnosis of HIV+ or AIDS in an infant is a confirmation of a positive diagnosis in the mother, the majority of whom are young single parents who are predominantly economically disadvantaged and for whom daily survival is a major concern (Carovano, 1994; Mays & Cochran, 1988; Stuber, 1992). Most mothers are unaware of their HIV+ status until their infants are diagnosed (Ybarra, 1991). Although the diagnosis in the infant is a confirmation of maternal infection, a positive diagnosis in the mother does not predict seropositivity in the infant. It has been reported that between 25 and 50% of infants born to HIV+ mothers become infected (Antoni et al., 1992; Birn, Santelli, & Burwell, 1994; James, 1988; Levine & Dubler, 1990; Stuber, 1992). The prognosis for children is poor. The younger the child is at the time of diagnosis, the shorter the child's survival time (Coleman, 1991, Stuber, 1992). Coleman reported a median survival time of 6.5 months for infants diagnosed under one year of age. Stuber (1992) reported an overall median survival time of 36 months from the time of diagnosis. However, many children who are infected perinatally with HIV+ are not diagnosed until early childhood or are treated effectively with drugs as infants and young children and live with HIV+ as a chronic terminal illness (Krieger, 1994; Stuber, 1992).

"It is estimated that more than three million women and children will die from AIDS during the 1990s, more than six times the number of those who died in the 1980s (Wiener, et al.,1994)." Although the reported cases of HIV+ and AIDS in women and children are increasing rapidly (Centers for Disease Control, 1996, 1995), a minimum of research has addressed the psychological responses of women in response to a diagnosis of HIV+ and/or AIDS for both themselves and their child. Similarly, a paucity of attention has been paid to the effects of treatment on women and children (Kalichman, 1995). Attention to vertically transmitted HIV+ or AIDS has focused mainly on demographics, the disease process itself, and on issues concerning methods of infection and risk, prevention, treatment, policy, and public attitudes (Silverman, 1993).

The psychological reactions to the diagnosis of a terminal illness have been shown to be parallel to psychological sequelae that accompany exposure to trauma (Doka, 1993; Rando, 1993). Many variables influence the human reaction to chronic terminal illness and to trauma. Specific psychological sequelae have been generally observed in response to both terminal illness and trauma. These are increased irritability and chronic anger, death anxiety, distancing and/or fear of intimacy and/or emotional numbness, and the increased need for emotional and physical support (Goodheart & Lansing, 1997; Rando, 1993; van der Kolk, 1987). Similar parental reactions have been documented as coexisting with pediatric terminal illness. Parents either prematurely detach emotionally from their sick and dying child, become preoccupied with their children, and/or intensify their attachment (Bowlby, 1980; Rando, 1986).

Living with chronic terminal illness requires coping with constant relapses and remissions and possible disfigurement, as well as numerous invasive medical procedures and heightened preoccupation with physical changes that are feared to be associated with relapse (Doka, 1993; Goodheart & Lansing, 1997; Rando, 1993). The vertical transmission of HIV+ or AIDS is unique in that both mother and child are living with acute or chronic terminal illness that is frequently experienced as being traumatic. Mothers are compelled to react and respond to their own illness while they simultaneously react and respond to their children's illness. Children who have not been infected by the AIDS virus are also parented by mothers with AIDS. Research has largely ignored the impact of a diagnosis of HIV+ or AIDS on the mother/child relationship. This study examined the psychological sequelae, as they impact maternal attachment, that result when women with AIDS live with their own chronic and potentially terminal illness while parenting children with AIDS, children whose seropositivity is uncertain and children who have not been infected by the virus.

OBJECTIVE

In this study, I examined the psychological literature that is associated with psychological trauma, resiliency, chronic illness, death and dying, complicated and anticipated mourning, and attachment. The intent of the research was to integrate these theories as they explain the feelings and behaviors of mothers with AIDS, who have children with AIDS, or with uncertain diagnoses, as well as to understand the relationship of mothers with their children who have not been infected by the virus. The psychological sequelae associated with the diagnosis of a life-threatening illness and the progressive psychological stages associated with the physiological progression of chronic terminal illness have been documented (Doka, 1993; Kubler-Ross, 1969). Differences in psychological sequelae have been found to be associated with the degree of disease symptomatology present (Doka, 1993; Kubler-Ross, 1969; Rando, 1984; Rando, 1986; Raphael, 1983; Sarwer & Crawford, 1994). Attachment between mother and child is supported when the mother experiences emotional support and a facilitating environment that enables her to focus on the reciprocal relationship that mother and child develop (Bowlby, 1973, 1980, 1982; Winnicott, 1965, 1987).

RATIONALE

Attachment between mother and child is a reciprocal process that is impacted when either mother or child has a fatal chronic illness. The diagnosis of a life threatening illness has been described as being traumatic and as a turning point in the individual's life (Doka, 1993). Living with chronic illness changes the roles and responsibilities within the family. The individual who is living with chronic illness frequently seeks reassurance and support from family members (Goodheart & Lansing, 1994). The anticipated death of oneself or another commonly impacts the relationship between the dying person and her/his loved ones (Doka, 1993, Parkes & Weiss, 1983; Rando, 1986, 1993) by intensifying the relationship or by causing intrapsychic premature separation. It was expected that attachment and concern would be exacerbated in cases of vertically transmitted AIDS or where the potential for transmission existed (i.e. during pregnancy or while awaiting diagnosis of seropositivity in infants). Parental loss of a child has been described as particularly intense, complicated and long-lasting (Rando, 1986, 1993). A correlation with the manifestation of the disease process and the psychological sequelae was anticipated to impact the participants' interpersonal relationships and ultimately the mother-child relationship. The impact of poverty, minority group status, chemical addiction, social, political and economic disenfranchisement and the stigma associated with HIV+ or AIDS was expected to impact the psychological sequelae as well.

PREMISES OF STUDY

This study was based on the following premises. The first premise was that the diagnosis of a life threatening illness is traumatic and can result in specific psychological symptoms and syndromes that correspond to the presence or absence of disease symptoms (Doka, 1993; Rando, 1993). The second premise was that the mother's psychological reaction to her own diagnosis and disease manifestation complicate her ability to simultaneously bond with and grieve for her dying child. This reaction, which has been described as anticipatory mourning (Rando, 1986, 1993), influences the mother's bereavement and can appear as indifference and detachment or enmeshment and preoccupation. The third premise was that womens' psychological reactions to the diagnosis and disease of HIV+/AIDS in themselves and their children are impacted by the unique concerns related to their gender and childbearing situations. Although the child's psychological reactions clearly impact the mother-child relationship and will be illuminated, the focus of the research was women who have been diagnosed with HIV+ or AIDS and who have potentially vertically transmitted this disease to their children.

STUDY SIGNIFICANCE

It is hoped that the implications of this study will enable psychologists and other health care providers with whom mothers and infants interact to have greater understanding and empathy for the observed behaviors and expressed feelings of the individuals who are diagnosed with this virus. As the feelings and opinions of the majority of women identified with HIV+ or AIDS have been neglected in the research on HIV+ or AIDS, it is hoped that this study will elucidate their voices. An understanding of the psychological processes that are inherent in the diagnosis of vertical transmission could result in the creation of psychological services and community programs that would assist mothers and children with HIV+ or AIDS as they navigate through their illnesses and in the world. Insight into the relational impact on mothers and children of living and dying with HIV+/AIDS could also facilitate

8

the development of services for children who are seronegative and who could potentially become AIDS orphans. Since a connection has been made between stress and the exacerbation of the AIDS disease process (Antoni et al., 1992), the establishment of these services and programs could reduce the amount of stress upon mothers with HIV+ and thereby extend their lives. An integrative conceptualization of the psychological sequelae and processes associated with vertically transmitted HIV+ or AIDS could enable professionals and health care workers to facilitate mothers' intrapsychic mourning of the losses associated with anticipated death of themselves and their children while simultaneously assisting them to remain connected and to direct more energy to their living as well as dying children. Facilitating the creation of larger psychological and physical support systems for mothers with AIDS will also enable them to continue to parent their healthy children in a nurturing supportive manner. Greater understanding of the psychological sequelae associated with vertically transmitted HIV+ or AIDS could also increase our knowledge and understanding of other congenitally transmitted diseases such as Tay Sachs and Huntingtons Chorea.

The results of this study could also broaden our understanding of the impact of the diagnosis of a life-threatening illness in mothers or children. In that the majority (75%) of the women with AIDS currently are African-American or Latina, the elucidation of the psychological processes that are inherent in these cultures with respect to attachment, trauma and mourning, and the differences if any, from those that are described in the literature review would facilitate the design of programs and services that are more culturally sensitive. Greater understanding of the psychological symptoms and processes associated with vertical transmission could also foster greater understanding of maternal responses to Fetal Alcohol Syndrome and Neonatal Abstinence Syndrome, two other conditions that affect infants and young children and are vertically transmitted. The research on the mother-child relationship in these two related areas is limited as well.

PILOT STUDY

This author conducted a pilot study on the psychological reactions of women who have vertically transmitted HIV+ or AIDS in Spring 1994. In that study, three women were interviewed; two of the women were African-American and one woman was White. The women were recruited by a social worker with whom they were being assisted at the Visiting Nurses Association.in a New England city. The design of the study was qualitative and open-ended questions were asked of the participants. All three were interviewed while their child was present. When asked, "What has your life been like since the diagnosis of HIV+?," the women freely described their shock at the diagnosis, their attempts to keep the diagnosis a secret from their child and from family members (even when disease symptoms were present), their hopes for their child's future, and the way in which the presence of HIV+ had impacted their lives, their children, and their relationship with their children

The interviews were transcribed verbatim and summarized into specific themes. The salient themes were:

1. Psychological denial was used when mother and child were asymptomatic.
2. The women who exhibited disease symptoms acknowledged the impact of HIV+/AIDS on their lives.
3. Emotional detachment marked responses of the mother who was most symptomatic and in the end stages of the physical disease process.
4. Hypervigilance about their child's health and treatment.
5. Intensification of relationship between mother and child when they were not experiencing end stage AIDS.
6. Guilt and remorse.
7. All were shocked when both they and their child were diagnosed with HIV+.
   a Even when the mother was aware of her HIV+ status prior to pregnancy, the risk of vertical transmission seemed small.
8. The time of diagnosis was reported as being the most stressful period.
9. Stress was associated with periods of remission and relapse.

10. Fear of disclosure and the resulting stigma.

II
Literature Review: HIV+/AIDS

HISTORY OF AIDS

AIDS in humans is believed to have first originated in Central Africa during the mid-1970s through contact with the African Green Monkey (Krieger & Appleman, 1994). The AIDS epidemic quickly spread throughout Africa, Asia, the Caribbean and Latin America. In the United States, between 1979 and 1981, 26 gay men in New York and five gay men in Los Angeles, who were previously healthy, exhibited rare opportunistic infections. In the two years since these men had become ill, ten had died. Noticing that these men were gay, the disease became associated with gay men. In August 1981, the Centers for Disease Control reported that five heterosexual people, including one woman, had been diagnosed with similar conditions (Levine, 1994). The incidence of the opportunistic infection in heterosexual men and women was initially ignored and the disease was identified as GRID or gay-related immunodeficiency "As the numbers of reported cases grew, the disease began to acquire its social identity as a new epidemic, a 'gay plague' (Fee & Krieger, 1994)."

Initially, AIDS appeared to be a disease of the United States, Western Europe and Australia where young men died in the prime of their life. A connection between the disease that quickly spread in Africa and that of industrialized countries was not initially made because in Africa, AIDS was a disease of heterosexuality and poverty (Fee & Krieger, 1994). The first cases of the previously unrecognized immunodeficiency disorder in adults and children were reported in the United States by the Centers for Disease Control in 1981 (Seibert & Olson, 1989). The etiology of the disease was unknown at this time.

Documentation of the disease in women and some children in 1982 caused the Centers for Disease Control to change the name of this disease to "acquired immunodeficiency syndrome" or AIDS (Seibert & Olson, 1989). The initial description emphasized the following criteria for diagnosis: that the person be diagnosed with an opportunistic infection or unusual malignancy indicative of underlying cellular immunodeficiency, that the person had no prior illnesses that predispose to immunodeficiency, that the person not be taking immunosuppressive drugs, and that a person with congenital immunodeficiency be excluded. In 1983, a retrovirus, initially called human T cell lymphotropic virus-III, was isolated from a patient with AIDS and identified as the cause of AIDS. This virus is now called human immunodeficiency virus-1 or HIV+ (Seibert & Olson, 1989). This definition did not describe the manifestations of AIDS in children (Fee & Krieger, 1994). The diagnosis of AIDS was initially made with the presence of a deteriorating immune system and specific opportunistic infections. In 1993, the definition of AIDS was revised. Individuals with HIV infection who are asymptomatic but receive a T-cell count of less than 200 currently meet the diagnostic criteria for AIDS (Kalichman, 1995). The updated case definition, defined by the Centers for Disease Control (1996) include diseases that are manifestations of HIV+/AIDS in women and children.

History of Pediatric AIDS

Many experts continued to deny the existence of AIDS in children until 1983 when the first cases studies were published which reported infants born to intravenous drug users or women with multiple sexual partners in New York and New Jersey (Seibert & Olson, 1989). These reports documented specific clinical features of AIDS-related infections in children, without a documented opportunistic infection. These features included recurrent bacterial infections and sepsis, failure to thrive, chronic diarrhea and persistent thrush. In June, 1985, the Centers for Disease Control revised the definition of AIDS to include clinical criteria for the diagnosis in children, the critical difference being the type of pneumonia that is not usually seen in adults but diagnostic of AIDS in children. In August, 1987, this definition was further revised and recognized immune defects seen only in children.

DEMOGRAPHICS OF AIDS

The demographical pattern of AIDS is distinct in developed and underdeveloped countries. High rates of AIDS affect Central Africa and Haiti, where the majority of people with AIDS are non-intravenous drug users and are heterosexuals, the male:female ratio reported at 1:1 (Krieger & Appleman, 1994). The majority of women with HIV+/AIDS in the United States contracted the virus through heterosexual transmission. Although the cases of heterosexual transmission are rising in the United States, the majority of cases have been identified in intravenous drug users or gay men (Krieger & Appleman, 1994). The Centers for Disease Control (CDC) currently (AIDS Weekly Surveillance Report, 1996) reports 293,433 cases of people living with AIDS in the United States: 69,151 of these cases were reported in 1996. Of the 69,151 cases reported in 1996, 678 were children with AIDS and 13,820 were women with AIDS. The CDC (1996) reports 3,983 women and 1,497 children under 12 years of age were diagnosed with HIV+ in 1996. Due to differences in the pediatric HIV+ classification used to report new cases and the classifications of pediatric HIV+ that physicians used to report new cases, and the classifications of pediatric HIV+ that physicians use to diagnose HIV+ infection in children, it is estimated that ". . . for every case of CDC-defined AIDS reported, there are four more children with other forms of HIV+ infection (Seibert & Olson, 1989)." Women currently account for 85,500 of the cumulative number of reported cases with 13,820 cases reported (or 20%of the reported cases) in 1996 (AIDS Weekly Surveillance Report, 1996).

Demographical Data about Women and AIDS

AIDS disproportionately affects African American, Latino (Levine & Dubler, 1990; Zucker & Gordon, 1988) and Haitian women (Krieger & Appleman, 1994). Women with HIV+ are mainly in their twenties and thirties, with about half being intravenous drug users, many of whom are single mothers (Levine & Dubler, 1990). Levine and Dubler (1990) report that the death rate among women due to HIV+ infection quadrupled between 1985 and 1988. The World Health Organization (Carovano, 1994) recognizes these figures as being lower than accurate due to worldwide underreporting of AIDS cases among women. In fact, Cohen (1993) reports that AIDS has become the leading cause of death for women between the ages of 15 and 44 since 1986 and, in some areas, has become the leading cause of death for African-American women. Approximately fifteen times as many women as men contract AIDS through heterosexual contact (Ybarra, 1991). Women can become infected by seminal fluid if they are partners of men who are bisexual, who have been infected by other women, or who are IV drug users (Olson, Huszti, Mason & Seibert, 1989). Armistead and Forehand (1995) report that the rate of male-to-female transmission by heterosexual contact has been reported to be 12 times more likely than female-to- male transmission. Non-drug using heterosexual women who live in poor inner-city neighborhoods, where seroprevalence is high, are more likely to have an HIV+ partner (Zuckerman & Gordon, 1988).

The largest populations of women and children with HIV+ or AIDS continue to live in metropolitan areas such as New York, Newark, and Miami. By 1988, 1,346 or 1.5% of the reported cases of AIDS were diagnosed in children younger than 13 years of age (Seibert & Olson, 1989). The majority of cases of vertically transmitted AIDS are caused by maternal intravenous drug use, in this country. However, the rate of women who have been infected through heterosexual contact has rapidly grown and the expectation is that the vertical transmission from this group of women will increase as well (Stuber, 1992).

MEDICAL ASPECTS OF AIDS

AIDS is caused by the human immunodeficiency virus or HIV+. A unique feature of HIV+ is that it can have an asymptomatic phase lasting as long as 10-15 years during which time the immune system is compromised and the individual is capable of transmitting the disease (Antoni, et al., 1992). HIV+ directly weakens and attacks the immune system by destroying the cells that are designed to recognize and destroy foreign elements (or viruses) in the body. With the destruction of these cells (called helper T-cells), multiple infections can enter the body without the activation of the immune system (Olson, Huszti, Mason & Seibert, 1989). As HIV+ disease progresses, the loss in immunocompetence leaves the individual susceptible to the presence of opportunistic infections that become the syndrome known as AIDS or acquired immunodeficiency syndrome. These opportunistic infections commonly include pneumocystisi carinii pneumonia, cryptococcal meningitis, and toxoplasmosis-related meningoencephalitis, candidal esophagitis, and herpes simplex encephalitis (Antoni et al., 1992). In recognition that the manifestation of AIDS in men and women can be different, the Centers for Disease Control (1996) added three additional clinical conditions to the case definition in 1993. These are pulmonary tuberculosis, recurrent pneumonia, and invasive cervical cancer. Many of the opportunistic infections characteristic of AIDS lead to progressive physical disfigurement and deterioration (Chesney & Folkman, 1994). Symptoms of AIDS include oral thrush, sleep disturbances, night sweats, rashes, diarrhea, wasting, dyspnea, musculoskeletal pain and neuropathy (Chesney & Folkman, 1994).

AIDS can be transmitted by the transfer of HIV+ infected seminal or vaginal fluids, through contact with infected blood (by intravenous drug use with infected needles) or perinatally from an infected mother to her developing child (Olson, Huszti, Mason & Seibert, 1989). Testing positive for HIV+ antibodies indicates that the individual has been exposed to HIV+ and can transmit the virus to others. Individuals who are tested as HIV+ may be healthy or may experience physical symptoms of the disease that would classify them as having AIDS-related complex or ARC (Antoni, 1992; Olson, Huszti, Mason & Seibert, 1989).

PSYCHOLOGICAL MANIFESTATIONS OF AIDS

Individuals with HIV+ or AIDS may experience emotional or personality changes as a result of the central nervous system deterioration that accompanies the disease. Seropositive individuals may become irritated and anxious when frustrated or overstimulated, and may experience short term memory impairment. These emotional and personality changes will impact the psychological manifestations of the disease process (Worden, 1991). Individuals may exhibit ". . . withdrawal and apathy, distractibility and agitation, emotional lability and angry outbursts, and the inability to sustain attention and affective states (Zegans, Gerhard & Coates, 1994, p. 158)." Although the way in which individuals respond to the diagnosis and disease process of HIV+ is unique, specific concerns are common. As people with cancer commonly experience, concerns about physical and cognitive deterioration, fear of rejection by partners, family and friends and the emotional sequelae associated with detection of the disease and resulting discrimination are common themes reported by both men and women (Zegans, Gerhard & Coates). Depression which is often accompanied by suicidal ideation is a very common problem for people with AIDS. Guilt about earlier behavior and the belief that the illness is a punishment are also common feelings. Internalized societal beliefs about sexual practices and orientations and substance abuse frequently stimulate feelings of guilt and/or regret in the person with AIDS (Zegans, Gerhard & Coates, 1994; Faltz, 1992). "Such beliefs may reflect certain moralistic attitudes of parts of the community, but may also reflect the patient's own intrapsychic beliefs and conflicts (Zegans, Gerhard & Coates, p. 153)."

PEDIATRIC AIDS

Diagnosis and Transmission

Children were previously diagnosed with AIDS if they were seropositive and had at least two serious bacterial infections, HIV+ wasting syndrome (severe weight loss with chronic diarrhea or unexplained fever) and HIV+-related encephalopathy (Seibert & Olson, 1989). The current pediatric classification system, revised in 1994, requires a single positive HIV detection test for a reportable AIDS diagnosis (Centers for Disease Control, 1996).

Vertical transmission of HIV-+ occurs through the placenta during the second and third trimesters of pregnancy and through blood and vaginal fluid at birth. It is possible that HIV may also be transmitted through breast milk. Transmission is most likely to occur when the mother has been recently infected or when she is more symptomatic (Kalichman, 1995). Although HIV+ infection occurs in 20% to 40% of infants born to mothers with AIDS, risk for perinatal HIV+ transmission has been reduced by administration of antiretroviral medications during pregnancy and to newborns (Kalichman). Currently, in most states all newborns are tested for the presence of HIV+ antibodies at birth. If these antibodies are present, the diagnosis of HIV+ in the mother is confirmed. The presence of HIV+ antibodies in the infant indicates that there is a 25% chance that the child is also HIV+ (Gorman, 1994). The diagnosis of pediatric AIDS is not clearly determined because of the presence of maternal antibodies in the infant's circulation. When the mother is HIV+, her antibodies will usually cross the placenta and be detected in the umbilical cord blood at birth. These antibodies can persist in the infant for several months, and on occasion, maternal HIV+ antibodies have been detected as late as 18 months of age. Maternal HIV+ antibodies can be detected whether or not the child is HIV+ (Seibert & Olson, 1989). As a result, unless clinical signs and symptoms of HIV+ are present in the child, the child cannot be diagnosed definitely seropositive until 15-18 months of age (Seibert & Olson, 1989). However, a test for the presence of HIV itself can be done earlier (Kalichman). Infants who have been vertically infected usually experience symptoms of HIV+ during their first year of life, usually at four to five months of age (Stuber, 1992).

Manifestation of Pediatric AIDS

AIDS in children manifests differently and proceeds at a faster rate of deterioration than in adults. The key difference in pediatric AIDS is a type of pulmonary disease that is called pulmonary lymphoid hyperplasia. This form of pneumonia, usually not seen in adults, produces hypoxemia (or an abnormally low concentration of oxygen in the blood) and subsequent morbidity (Seibert & Olson, 1989). Neurological symptoms have been found in as many as 70% of pediatric AIDS patients. Early neurological symptoms of HIV+ infection include headaches, encephalitis, aseptic meningitis, ataxia, dementia, and developmental delays (Olson, Huszti, Mason & Seibert, 1989). The rate of neurological impairment varies in children, but seems to be related to the child's age at symptom onset and the length of time the child has been diagnosed with AIDS. Some children display a rapid deterioration in developmental milestones while others show a slower decline in cognitive and motor skills (Olson, Huszti, Mason & Seibert, 1989). Early diagnosis and initiation of antiviral treatments has delayed disease progression in many children. Intravenous administration of AZT has been found to produce significant improvement in symptoms and neurodevelopment (Stuber, 1992).

WOMEN AND AIDS

Sexual Inequality

Carovano (1994) asserts that sexual inequality places women at greater risk for AIDS. She states that women who attempt to introduce condoms into a heterosexual relationship are often seen as being overly prepared for sex or may even be suspected of being HIV+ themselves. "For all women, condoms and non-penetrative sex . . . both require male cooperation, which implicitly means male control (Carovano, 1994, p. 120)." In a consentual relationship, when a couple desires to conceive a child, the lack of available methods of protection, other than abstinence or condoms, leave the couple without protection from AIDS transmission (Zuckerman & Gordon, 1988).

Manifestations of AIDS in Women

Some differences exist in the way in which HIV+ manifests in women, with some evidence that reports shorter survival times for women than men (Zuckerman & Gordon, 1988; Antoni et al., 1992; Ybarra, 1991). Women are more likely to get Pneumocystus Carinii Pneumonia, while men are more likely to get Kaposi's Sarcoma, which offers a longer life prognosis (Ybarra, 1991). Research has linked increased stress with exacerbation of HIV+ (Antoni, et al., 1992; Chesney & Folkman,

1994). Antoni et al., (1992) assert that the deleterious living conditions with which most women with HIV+ live, place them at greater risk for multiple chronic psychosocial stressors that exacerbate the disease process. These include chronic financial hassles, drug and alcohol dependency, poor social networks, medical problems, and a general feeling of helplessness and powerlessness. These stressors may interact to aggravate a perceived loss of control resulting in the previously mentioned affective, neuroendocrine, and immunological changes (Antoni et al., 1992 p. 57).

MOTHERS AND AIDS

Kurth (1993) maintains that identifying HIV infection compels women to adapt to the information with the grieving process. "Little has been written about the interaction between grief and pregnancy, yet grief may have important implications for women with HIV infection (Kurth, p. 109)." Citing research with womens' psychological and behavioral reactions to the death of a parent, she suggests that pregnancy frequently fulfills loss-related needs (Kurth, 1993).

Pregnancy

Pregnancy and parenting associated psychological stressors that are unique to women include the decision to maintain the pregnancy, the psychological stress of pregnancy and labor and the uncertainty of perinatal transmission outcome. When seropositivity is not conclusive following birth, mothers face an extended period of uncertainty while they await their child's diagnostic outcome (Sherr, 1995). This potentially traumatic situation is exacerbated when the diagnosis is positive. Since the disease process in seropositive infants is usually faster and more intense, ". . . parents face enormous psychological trauma in the presence of an ill, ailing or dying child (Sherr, p. 56)." Caring for their ill and/or dying children is complicated by the fact that by caring for their children, seropositive mothers ". . . must observe the dying process that likely forecasts their own fate (Armistead & Forehand, 1995, p. 246)." Pregnancy itself is associated with impaired immunological function. The physiological changes associated with pregnancy are thought, by some, to exacerbate immune system suppression in a woman with AIDS and, as a result, accelerate the progression of viral infections (Antoni et al., 1992, Armistead & Forehand, 1995). Physical and psychological stressors commonly associated with the postpartum period can exacerbate the disease progression and can be aggravated by the impact of HIV+ status of the infant and the added stress associated with caring for a potentially ill child. The fact that seropositive mothers are frequently the only care giver or the primary care giver and that seropositive mothers report neglecting their own needs to take care of their children, increases the likelihood for accelerated AIDS progression (Armistead & Forehand, 1995; Geballe, Gruendel, & Andiman, 1995). In fact, women with AIDS report that they neglect their own health needs in order to focus on their children's needs. Ignoring their own needs, the disease process itself and the commonly experienced social isolation frequently result in extreme exhaustion for women with AIDS (Geballe, Gruendel, & Andiman, 1995).

Women may knowingly become pregnant, when aware of their HIV+ status, because they view childbearing as a cultural expectation and a sign of worth (Ybarra, 1991) or as a chance to have a part of them survive (Stuber, 1992). Women may perceive the benefits of becoming pregnant or of maintaining a pregnancy as far outweighing any risks. These perceived benefits can include escape from an abusive parental household, becoming part of a social support group of other mothers, obtaining financial assistance, or the belief in leaving behind a legacy of a child after death (Antoni et al., 1992).

Prenatal Knowledge of Serostatus

When women become aware of their seropositive status prior to delivery, they may choose to continue the pregnancy because they believe the risk factor to be low. While research (James, 1988; Kalichman, 1995; Stuber, 1992) does indicate a risk factor of approximately 25%-40% for infant infection when the mother is HIV+, and as low as 8% when the mother receives intense AZT treatment during pregnancy (Armistead & Forehand, 1995), there is no known way of ascertaining the infant's serostatus prior to delivery. The perceived risks of daily survival issues such as poverty and shootings, and the lack of resources to make alternative choices, outweigh the fact that their child has a 20-40% chance of being diagnosed with HIV+ (Armistead & Forehand, 1995; Levine & Dubler, 1990; Ybarra, 1991).

> Risks that are immediate, catastrophic and against which clear action
> can be taken are treated differently from risks that are long term . . .
> and offer few or unacceptable preventative actions, regardless of the
> statistical level of risk (Levine & Dubler, 1990, p. 342).

Mothers' Feelings While Pregnant

Although Birn, Santelli and Burwell (1994) assert that the mother's concern for her own serostatus and that of her unborn child may not be a priority when living in an atmosphere where the hold on basic survival needs is fragile, Septimus (1990) and Melvin and Sherr (1993) describe anguish, guilt, and shame experienced by mothers who have vertically transmitted HIV+. Economic difficulties did not preclude attachment or emotion in these mothers. Although perceived risk may be comparatively small and survival issues may be paramount, mothers frequently choose to continue their pregnancy mainly or solely due to religious and/or moral beliefs that conflict with pregnancy termination (Armistead & Forehand, 1995).

Dubler and Levine (1990) and Mays and Cochran (1988) dispute the notion that has been advanced that testing during pregnancy to ascertain HIV+ status of the mother and subsequent elective abortions are methods of preventing pediatric AIDS. African Americans in inner cities, one of the higher prevalence HIV+ groups, are more likely to delay prenatal care until the third trimester or to have no prenatal care at all (Mays and Cochran, 1988), thus eliminating the possibility of elective abortion. Moreover, the cultural value of children for Latina and African American women must not be minimized (Mays and Cochran, 1988). When prenatal care is obtained in the first trimester and seropositivity in the mother is established, lack of Medicaid funding for elective abortions may preclude pregnancy termination even if the woman should choose to abort (Ybarra, 1991). Sherr (1993) asserts that while early testing allows for prophylactic treatment and better management of infections, maternal psychological trauma is exacerbated. She maintains that testing for HIV during pregnancy can trigger a psychological crisis as women potentially experience extreme levels of guilt and anger, as well as agonizing periods of uncertainty as they pass from childbirth to motherhood. This trauma begins with the anticipated results of the testing and continues as the mothers wait to learn if the infant is seropositive.

> Acute anxiety is common and may manifest itself in sudden bursts of panic. Depression can often set in when seropositive women have to contemplate their own future and the fact that their illness may be passed on to their baby or may leave their baby without a parent (Sherr, 1993, p. 59).

Womens' Self-esteem and AIDS

Ybarra (1991) reports that concomitant with a diagnosis of HIV+ is the loss of health, body image and childbearing potential and psychological responses that are specific to women with AIDS. She reports that fear of transmitting the disease to husbands or partners, fear of progressive disfigurement, deterioration and ultimately death, and guilt over past behaviors are common responses to a diagnosis of HIV+ in women. Fearing rejection and/or abandonment over issues associated with the disease process or as a result of the stigma of the diagnosis itself, women frequently withdraw from the physical comfort of relationships. "Intimacy is another concern for seropositive women who may feel sexually dirty and unloved (Ybarra, p. 186)." Further physical and emotional withdrawal may occur if the woman believes that she is unable to maintain a sexual relationship.

> For some women, sex is the only way that they know to experience intimacy and they may be afraid to tell their partners that they need to change their sexual practices. They may fear rejection and

abandonment and their fears may not be unwarranted. (Ybarra, 1991, p. 186).

Feelings of anger and betrayal may impact intimate relationships if the woman became infected with HIV+ through heterosexual transmission and believes that her partner concealed his serostatus from her or was unaware of his own risk.

When the woman herself is an intravenous drug user, the constant focus on obtaining heroine, coupled with the alternating cycle of intoxication and withdrawal, can exacerbate the symptoms of the disease process while simultaneously causing the woman to deny the concomitant implications (Faltz, 1992). Conversely, the shock of the diagnosis and the difficulty of living with a chronic disease can increase drug and alcohol dependency as a way of temporarily numbing the physical and emotional pain or quieting the stress associated with HIV+ (Antoni, et al., 1992). For some intravenous drug users, pregnancy may serve as a motivator to recover from drug addiction (Armistead & Forehand, 1995).

Women who are seropositive must confront unique issues that can increase their isolation and their own stress levels. In order to protect their children from anticipated grief and stigmatization, they may chose not to reveal their HIV+ status, but live in fear of disclosure. "A mother may be concerned that her children will feel that she 'did something wrong' to contract the illness, which may result in the children feeling bad about themselves or rejecting their mother (Armistead & Forehand, 1995, p. 243)." In addition to the previous reasons cited for secrecy, mothers may guard their seropositivity from their children out of fear that their children will disclose their HIV+ status to others. Future planning for their children may be difficult, if not impossible, if mothers are unable to accept the implications of their diagnosis and disease process. "We have found that mothers frequently comment that they hope to live long enough to see their child finish high school or marry (Armistead & Forehand, 1995, p. 245)." When mothers experience anticipatory grief and intrusive thoughts and feelings about their own deterioration and death, they commonly become depressed and highly symptomatic, during which time it is extremely difficult to nurture children. However, Armistead & Forehand did report that mothers disclosed to them that they experienced increased attachment and paid greater attention to their children following their diagnosis of HIV+. "Mothers who are seropositive have discussed with us their intention to make the most of the time that they have left with their child (Armistead & Forehand, 1995, p. 245)."

RESEARCH WITH WOMEN

James Study

James (1988) interviewed fifteen women who were referred for psychiatric evaluations in pregnancy following the diagnosis of HIV seropositivity, and described their psychological reactions. The interviews occurred either in consultation during an obstetric hospitalization or during an intake evaluation at a psychiatric-obstetric clinic. None of the women exhibited any evidence of AIDS, ARC, or HIV+ encephalopathy during the period of time that the interviews were conducted. The women ranged in age from 17-32 years old. Eleven of the women were African-American and four of the women were white. Seven women most likely acquired the infection from intravenous drug use, five women used intravenous drugs and also had sexual contact with a high-risk man (a man who engaged in intravenous drug use and/or was bisexual), two women had sexual contact with a high-risk male alone and one woman acquired HIV+ from a blood transfusion. Five women had partners or children who were diagnosed with AIDS or HIV+. The 2 1/2 year old child of one woman died of AIDS 3 months before the initial interview and the 2 year old child of another woman was diagnosed as having AIDS. Two women experienced the death of a partner or husband; one man died one month before the interview and the other died 4 months after the woman delivered her baby. One partner was tested HIV+ after the woman was diagnosed. The diagnosis of AIDS in a 2 year old child of one of the women resulted in a positive diagnosis for both the mother and her partner.

All fifteen women were diagnosed with either an adjustment disorder (53.3%), a mood disorder (20%), or a personality disorder

(73.3%). Thirteen of the woman (86.7%) were also diagnosed with substance abuse or dependence. James states that adaptation to the diagnosis of HIV+ in pregnancy is impaired by the coexistence of a psychiatric diagnosis and substance abuse disorder. He reported that women with dual diagnoses frequently increase their drug or alcohol use after a seropositivity diagnosis. James further noted that the abuse of drugs could complicate the pregnancy, result in multiple problems for the children, and result in affective symptoms in the mother. James stated that "After delivery these mothers often bond poorly with their infants, resulting in potential neglect or abuse (James, 1988, p. 314)." He also reported that when women have comorbid diagnoses as well as histories of substance abuse, they are less likely to work through the processes of anticipatory grief and ". . . may instead become violent or suicidal, demonstrate hostility and belligerence toward hospital personnel, and are often noncompliant with medical care (James, p. 313)." However, James also reported that most of the women that he interviewed reported feeling saddened by the anticipated grief of their surviving children as well as experiencing feelings of fear, anger, shame and depression as a result of their seropositivity status. Many of the women expressed ". . . remorse, guilt, and anxious anticipation about the pregnancy. Some fantasized about, . . . 'watching the baby suffer and die.'(James, p. 313)." One woman whose child had recently died as a result of AIDS reported experiencing recurrent nightmares about the death.

Themes from a Support Group for Parents

An open support group for parents and caretakers of children with HIV+ was conducted at The New York Hospital Pediatric Clinic from February 1987 to February 1988. The clinic is a treatment and assessment center for the care of children with HIV+. By May 1992, 125 families with children with HIV+ had been followed by the center(Mayers & Spiegel, 1992). The majority of the children (85%) had at least one parent with a history of intravenous drug use. Regular group attendance was not required or requested and parents were encouraged to bring their children to the meetings. Although 10 members attended at varying times throughout the year, the average attendance consisted of 5 members. The members of the group were described (Mayers & Spiegel) as experiencing chronic problems associated with poverty such as inadequate housing, transportation limitations, limited finances, and other illnesses in addition to AIDS. Most parents attended the support group only if they had a clinic appointment on the same day, or lived nearby.

Guilt, fear, anger, isolation and loss of control were salient themes of the group. Many mothers expressed guilt and shame due to their own behaviors and the manner of disease transmittal. "One mother reported that every day she awakened so riddled with guilt for having abused drugs and transmitting the virus to her child that she felt 'like jumping off a bridge'(Mayers & Spiegel, p. 187)." Other mothers expressed feeling like "'lepers' (Mayers & Spiegel, p. 187)" when their hospitalized children were placed in isolation or when medical staff used excessive precautions in their care taking. Other mothers expressed feelings of isolation and detachment from their children's fathers. One woman described her child's father as avoiding acceptance of the diagnosis and disease process and its effect on her emotional equilibrium. "His inability to face their son's illness compounded her sense of isolation, shame, and guilt (Mayers & Spiegel, p. 187)." Mothers expressed distress at their childrens' slow deterioration and poor quality of life and anger at excessive and evasive medical procedures.

> One mother explained how she had curtailed a doctor's repeated and unsuccessful attempts to draw blood from her daughter. The group encouraged her right to speak up, feeling that the distress a test causes the child may be greater than its medical benefits (Mayers & Spiegel, 1992, p. 188).

Other group themes included fear of contagion to other non-infected children and the need to maintain some hope in order to face AIDS-related issues in the future. As children of group members died, the group also served as a bereavement support group for mothers who were not able to mourn publicly because of the secrecy that frequently surrounds pediatric AIDS (Mayers & Spiegel).

Videotaped Messages to Children

Twenty women with HIV+ were offered the opportunity to make a videotape of themselves for their children in order to facilitate the grieving process and to create legacies or memories of themselves for their children (Taylor-Brown & Wiener, 1993). When videotaped, the mothers expressed sorrow and anger over their inability to care for their children in the future and expressed their despair and suffering over the loss of this relationship. Many attempted to relieve any guilt that the child may feel following her/his mother's death and expressed their own feelings of guilt and shame regarding the way in which they contracted HIV+ and the stigma associated with the disease itself (Taylor-Brown & Wiener, 1993).

Social Support and Clinical Outcome

In an ongoing study of mothers with HIV+, Andrews, Williams and Neil (1993) attempted to ascertain the relationship between the amount of social support that was reported by the mothers, their use of clinical services and clinical outcomes for themselves and their children. The criteria for participation in the study was a diagnosis of HIV+ and to have completed at least one pregnancy while seropositive. (The women may have learned of their serostatus following delivery). As of February 1, 1993, 80 mothers had participated in the study. The average age of the participants was 30 years, with the sample consisting of 40 African-Americans (56%), 13 Latinas (18%), and 18 Whites (25%). Twenty-five women (37%) were currently using drugs and/or alcohol and 26 (38%) used drugs only in the past. The women who participated in the study took part in two separate interviews that were 4 to 6 months apart. At the first interview, a general questionnaire was administered. This questionnaire included questions regarding demographics and whether the woman knew of her serostatus at the time of her child/children's births. The Norbeck Social Support Questionnaire and the Addiction Severity instrument were administered as well. The second interview consisted of open-ended questions and a readministration of the Norbeck Social Support Questionnaire (Andrews et al., 1993).

The preliminary findings of this study indicated that one-third of the mothers reported that they depended on support from children under 16 years of age, and in fact, listed children 8 years old or younger as major sources of support (Andrews et al., 1993). The mothers revealed that the child's presence decreased their feelings of isolation and gave them a reason to live, by focusing on the child's needs instead of their own situation. The need to maintain connections with social support systems for the benefit of their child/children forced the women to engage with others in the outside world. Providing adequate care for their children, especially when the children were seropositive, seemed to positively impact the self esteem of the women who were interviewed. Lastly, mothers reported that the presence of their children motivated them to refrain from engaging in the high risk behaviors associated with intravenous drug use (Andrews et al.).

Although many mothers in this study reported that their children were supportive to them, their relationship with their children also proved to be bittersweet. The women expressed feelings of anxiety about their surviving children's future and fear for their health. In addition, they reported that the energy used to care for their seropositive child was a heavy drain on them. In that the majority of mothers were single parents, the need to be the primary and sole caretaker of a seropositive child precluded any privacy for the mother. Obtaining child care when needed was difficult and exacerbated by the need, expressed by some mothers, to disclose the child's HIV+ status so that the caretaker could take the necessary precautions. Lastly, the anger that some children expressed over their parents' terminal illness was difficult for mothers to endure (Andrews, et al., 1993).

Qualitative analysis of the data indicated a strong attachment between mothers and children. The authors inferred that the mother-child attachment might form "the underlying matrix of life for many of the women . . . (Andrews et al., 1993, p. 195)." One mother described her relationship with her daughter as "'My daughter . . . she's my heart.'(Andrews et al., p. 195)." Even when mothers and children lived apart, the mothers expressed feelings of strong attachment towards their children, viewing themselves and their children as part of each other (Andrews et al.). Incarcerated women who participated in the study reported that the psychological attachment to their child enabled them to endure prison life. One woman described using extreme measures in order to visit her newborn child after her cesarian delivery and return to prison one week later. "'I had to get hysterical, scream, cry, throw my tray across the room before they would take me. I just needed to be with my baby' (Andrews et al., p. 195)." Another mother described her intense attachment to her son and her willingness to test his medication on herself. "'They want to put him on DDI. The AZT is making him too anemic. I'm going to try the DDI dose they want him on first before they give it to him. . . . so I'll know what side effects he'll get from the DDI' (Andrews et al., p. 195)."

Most mothers who participated in the study (66%) did not disclose their own diagnosis to their children due to anxiety and fear related to the stigma and resulting isolation associated with HIV+ and AIDS upon disclosure (Andrews et al., 1993). Mothers reported extreme concern over maintaining the secrecy of their seropositivity status and concern over when their own physical condition would deteriorate to the extent that disclosure would be inevitable. Some thought that discontinued contact with their child might be preferable for the child than watching her/his mother deteriorate and die (Andrews et al.).

Care Giving Stress and Pediatric AIDS

The HIV+ disease creates stresses for parents who may need care and nurturing themselves as well as fulfilling a parenting and care giving role for their sick children. Parents frequently focused their attention on their children's needs, neglecting their own health and emotional needs (Melvyn & Sherr, 1993; Geballe, Gruendel, & Andiman, 1995). Melvyn and Sherr conducted case studies of 18 children who were seropositive as a result of vertical transmission and described specific factors that impacted parenting when both mother and child were HIV+. They concluded that the emotional consequences of HIV+ that include guilt, anxiety, panic, mood fluctuations, grief, fear, uncertainty and secrecy were salient factors. Financial concerns and lack of social support exacerbated the difficulties that mothers faced, which included caring for their sick child as they themselves experienced periods of tiredness and lack of energy as a result of their disease process. Developmental delays in their children complicated and were complicated by the recurring painful procedures and hospitalizations that the children endured while they were cared for by their mothers. Lastly, Melvin and Sherr found that the stress caused by frequent hospitalizations and medical procedures was increased when language barriers existed between medical care givers and mothers and children.

PSYCHOLOGICAL AND SOCIOLOGICAL ISSUES

The psychological and social issues confronting families with seropositive mothers and children are more complex than those of other childhood chronic and life-threatening illnesses because pediatric AIDS occurs mainly in areas of extreme poverty where social support is minimal due to the stigma of the disease (Septimus, 1990). Families are impacted by the intertwining stressors of the diagnosis, the disease process, the treatment and ultimately death. The stigma of the illness, which usually results in the unwillingness to share the diagnosis with family and friends, further overwhelms coping capacities and pushes families into crisis. The resulting social isolation that families feel is compounded by the frequent decision to keep the diagnosis from the child so that a "conspiracy of silence" exists within and without the home (Septimus, 1990, p. 95).

> Although the initial shock, anger, and chaos occur with the diagnosis, parents experience continuous fear, disbelief, anxiety, pain, stress, and feelings of being on an emotional roller coaster (Septimus, 1990, p. 94).

Many mothers who vertically transmitted HIV+ verbalize feelings of helplessness as a result of their traumatic lives (living with losses, poverty, drug addiction, violence, and abuse). The hopelessness that the women feel ultimately precipitates depression (Septimus, 1990; Brown & Harris, 1978). In addition to depression resulting from the diagnosis of HIV+ in themselves and their child, many mothers experience chronic premorbid depression resulting from the multiple problems and difficulties that they encounter daily. The depression is exacerbated by the guilt parents feel over the illness of their child and their own seropositivity status and the feelings of self-blame that they experience for failing to protect their children. The use of intravenous drugs frequently results in criminal involvement and becomes another stressor and possible source of depression (Septimus, 1990).

CULTURAL FACTORS

Latina/Latino Culture, Religion and Family Values

The majority of participants in this study were Latina women and they identified themselves with the social and spiritual values of their culture. A brief description of these values will elucidate the construct from which they navigated in the world.

Maternal Roles

Julia (1989) and Ramos-McKay, Comas-Diaz, and Rivera (1988) describe salient themes in the psychosocial development of Puerto Rican women as being focused on what they call "familism," or the cultural expectation that women (regardless of their economic or professional position) will place family needs unconditionally above their own. They reported that women commonly derive self-fulfillment through care taking roles and close family attachments. In this regard, infants born with congenital anomalies or with chronic disease can dramatically decrease maternal self- esteem during the initial postpartum period (Coll, Escobar, Cebollero, & Valcarcel, 1989).

Religion

Most Latino and Latinas in the United States are Roman Catholics (Irish, Lundquist & Nelsen, 1993). Representations of saints are commonly found in homes and families commonly light candles and pray to these statues. Catholic beliefs are often mingled with traditional cultural beliefs, that emphasize holy places, miracles and the need for penitence. For Christian Latins, death is not final. "Dying is seen not as an end but as a beginning, a passage from one state to another . . . (Irish, Lundquist & Nelsen, p. 204)." A close balance, therefore, is maintained between the present life and the one beyond. Mainstream Latino and Latina (or Puerto Rican) individuals believe that whatever God wants is expected to be followed. In that the belief system maintains that the soul becomes a part of the person at the moment of conception, abortions are generally not sanctioned (Irish, Lundquist & Nelsen).

CARE GIVERS AND AIDS

Stress

Women who have vertically transmitted AIDS care for children with AIDS. Caring for a person with AIDS has been found to be extremely stressful (Frierson, Lippman, & Johnson, 1987; Giucquinta, 1989; Rando, 1993; Silverman, 1993). The descriptions of psychological sequelae reported by family members and health care providers parallel those required for a diagnosis of posttraumatic stress disorder (Silverman, 1993). Health care providers report high levels of AIDS related nightmares, irritability, physical exhaustion, emotional numbing and detachment, and recurrent intrusive thoughts and dreams of HIV+ related care activities (Silverman). Giacquinta (1989) interviewed 45 family members from 27 families where at least one adult family member was seropositive. Themes of anticipatory grief, family exile and isolation, suicidal ideation, revulsion, anger, and guilt emerged (Giacquinta). Feelings of helplessness, depression and grief have also been reported (Frierson, Lippman, & Johnson, 1987). "Grieving was especially intense among parents, many of whom remarked that they had never expected to outlive their children (Frierson,Lippman, & Johnson, p. 67)."

Family Crisis

Families initially confront the diagnosis of AIDS as an acute family crisis where the members are mobilized and anticipate the diagnosed individual's death (Cates, Graham, Boeglin, & Tielker, 1990). After the initial crisis, when the person with AIDS recovers some degree of health, the family experiences the additional stress of adapting to the care of a chronically ill member. "Chronic illness usually causes anatomical and physiological changes, alternating periods of stability and crisis, need for care, low probability of improvement, and decreased life span . . . (Cates et al., 1990, p. 196)." The family members may not be able to express their grief at the current and future losses that they experience, in addition to their reactions to caring for a chronically ill individual due to the shame, guilt, and secrecy surrounding HIV+/AIDS. Without the ability to openly express grief and receive support, the normal grief process, which entails the working through or processing of the grief, is precluded (Cates et al.).

Forty-three mothers were interviewed twenty-four to thirty-seven months following the death of their sons. Those who cared for their sons full-time exhibited a cluster of symptoms that are associated with posttraumatic stress disorder (Trice, 1988). These symptoms included night terrors, outbursts of uncharacteristic violence, panic attacks, interpersonal difficulties and problems with attachment, and psychosomatic complaints. The majority of mothers (89%) were very angry as contrasted with mothers who had not cared for their sons where only 21% were angry (Trice, 1988).

CHRONIC/TERMINAL ILLNESS

Studies on Parental Responses to Chronic /Terminal Illness

As previously noted, the diagnosis of HIV+ in an infant is an automatic indicator of seropositivity in the mother. The use of new medications (AZT, DDI) has increased the length of time, in general, from the diagnosis of HIV+ (and a more asymptomatic period) to the disease progression resulting in AIDS. With these medications, the disease has become a chronic, although terminal, illness. Although there is uncertainty as to the exact causes, womens' life span, from the time of diagnosis of HIV+, is shorter then mens'. It has been speculated that factors that include the unique stressors of loving and caring for a child who is herself/himself HIV+ exacerbate the disease process in the mother. The process of pregnancy and delivery, and the associated psychological stressors and physiological changes, can also impact the

fact that men with AIDS live longer than women with AIDS. The
HIV+/AIDS disease process in children is different from either men or
women. For the most part, the asymptomatic period during the initial
HIV+ diagnosis, that can last up to ten years in adults, is almost non-
existent in children. As Stuber (1992) reported, the average length of
life after a diagnosis of pediatric AIDS is 36 months. Thus, when a
mother has vertically transmitted AIDS to her child, both mother and
child will grapple with the physiological and psychological problems
that are unique for each, and at the same time, inherent with this
chronic and terminal disease. While chronically ill and possibly dying
herself, the mother will need to attach to and care for her sick child
while she simultaneously anticipates and watches that child's
deterioration and death.

The diagnosis of a terminal illness in a child is traumatic for the
parent. Although the demographics and availability of social support
are different, the diagnosis of childhood leukemia can be compared to a
childhood diagnosis of HIV+. In both situations, children are diagnosed
with a terminal and chronic illness. In both, parents must
simultaneously anticipate the death of their child while intensifying
their emotional attachment and care taking. Neonatal Abstinence
Syndrome and Fetal Alcohol Syndrome are both vertically transmitted,
as in the case of HIV+/AIDS, and cause the infants to be born with
physical or neurological anomalies. These syndromes can also impact
the mother/child relationship because the child is born sick and unable
to engage optimally in a reciprocal relationship with the mother.

Childhood Leukemia

Although the demographics are different, the psychological crisis
caused by the diagnosis of childhood leukemia is similar to pediatric
AIDS in that the disease is terminal and marked by relapses and
remissions that can be prolonged and of variable intensity (Futteran, E.
D. & Hoffman, I., 1973).

Futterman and Hoffman (1973) interviewed 45 parents of children
with leukemia at various points of their child's illness over a six year
period. The parents were middle-class or lower-middle class residents
of a suburban community in Illinois. In this sample, the diagnosis of

leukemia resulted in an emotional crisis for the parents, which was characterized by marked internal turmoil and interpersonal disequilibrium. From their observations (Futterman & Hoffman), they concluded that the diagnosis of leukemia in their child compelled parents to adapt to conflicting tasks. As the parents anticipated the child's death and mourned their ultimate loss, they simultaneously maintained hope for the child's recovery. This hope gradually deteriorated as the parents became more aware of the child's terminal condition as the time of death neared. They concluded that as the parents allowed themselves to become more aware of their child's impending death, they withdrew emotional investment in the child. They oscillated between clinging and distancing until after their child died (Futterman & Hoffman). The onset of childhood leukemia assaulted the parents' cognitive assumption that they would be able to protect their child. Once this assumption was assaulted, parents felt extremely anxious about the unknown future/fate of themselves and their other children and became hypervigilant in their care taking. The quest for knowledge about the disease and for resources with which to fight the illness, enabled them to experience mastery and reduced their anxiety for a short time. The maintenance of interpersonal equilibrium further bolstered their feelings of control. They accomplished stabilization by adhering to familiar routines, continuing the family's usual patterns of interactions, and by reaching out for emotional supports. They further strove to maintain this equilibrium by monitoring and regulating their emotions.

> Erecting a facade of calm acceptance was used for concealing anguish, protecting others, protecting themselves, and preserving functioning. Parents usually avoided crying in front of the children, minimized displaying anxiety in the presence of neighbors and relatives, shielded the physician from their rage, and underplayed their fears and doubts . . . (Futterman & Hoffman, 1973, pp. 137-8).

Although most parents strove to prolong their child's life, they also longed to be relieved of their burdens and simultaneously wished to end their child's suffering, causing conflicting feelings as their child's death approached (Futterman & Hoffman).

Catastrophic Childhood Illness

Thirty-three children and thirty-three mothers were observed at the City of Hope Medical Center over a 26 month period (Natterson, 1973). The children ranged in age from infants to 13 years old and were diagnosed with fatal leukemia, cancer or blood disease. The mothers ranged in age from 24 to 45 years old. During the course of their illness, the children were separated from their mothers, experienced traumatic procedures and were exposed to the death of other children. Natterson concluded that when a child survived more than four months from the time of terminal prognosis, the mother exhibited a "triphasic response (Natterson, p. 122)." During the initial phase, denial and guilt were the predominant emotions. Regression and identification with the child were evident during this phase. In the intermediate phase, the mothers directed their efforts towards realistic resources that could possibly prolong their child's life. In the terminal phase, the mother's energies decathected from her child (Natterson, 1973).

Bowlby (1980) documented a series of empirical studies conducted by the National Institute of Mental Health that chronicled parents' reactions to their child's diagnosis of terminal leukemia. The research sample consisted of parents, between the ages of 23-49, who had experienced the death of a child as a result of childhood leukemia. The childrens' ages ranged from 1 1/2 years old to 16 years old at the time of death. Although gender differences were not indicated in the research findings, it is noted that the sample was comprised of 20% more mothers than fathers. The interviewers were concerned with the way in which the parents perceived their child's illness, the way in which they coped with the fatal diagnosis, and the manner in which they had coped with their child's death.

The research findings indicated that psychological mourning began at the time of the diagnosis. The way in which the parents responded initially determined the manner in which they would respond throughout the disease process. Parents reported that they were initially stunned by the diagnosis. An initial phase of numbing, punctuated by outbursts of anger, characterized the initial period following the diagnosis. During this period, parents commonly disbelieved the diagnosis and prognosis, utilizing a great deal of energy attempting to disprove the physicians. As they tried to deny the diagnosis, they were confronted with physicians who encouraged them to disclose the child's illness to her/him. The research revealed that failure to accept the diagnosis frequently resulted in failure to comply with the prescribed therapeutic program (Bowlby, 1980).

The majority of the parents appeared to accept the diagnosis and its implications but later revealed that it had taken days to sink in. While they attempted to psychologically integrate the implications of the diagnosis and prognosis, they reported feeling emotionally numb, frequently behaving in a detached manner and giving the impression of unconcern (Bowlby, 1980). Gradual detachment of emotional investment was reported when the child's illness continued for 3-4 months. Rising hopes became dashed and the parent came to accept the diagnosis, anticipating the child's death. Resignation about the fatal prognosis ensued. Bowlby (1980) reported that bereavement was muted when anticipation of the death had exceeded 4 months, indicating a detachment of emotional attachment prior to the child's death. Those who continued to disbelieve the diagnosis did not engage in anticipatory mourning (Bowlby, 1980).

Bereavement responses were recorded for this group of parents six months after the death of their child (Bowlby, 1980). The responses were divided between those who freely expressed their grief, displaying intense affect, and those who expressed no sadness. The accounts of the parents who had expressed no sadness suggested that they had engaged in little active grieving since their child's death. "Reminders of the child had been put away and both thoughts and talk about him avoided (Bowlby, 1980, p. 120)." The conclusion of the study indicated that parents' reactions to the loss were greatly dependent on spousal, familial and social support (Bowlby, 1980).

GENETICALLY TRANSMITTED DISORDERS

Tay-Sachs Disease and Huntingtons Disease

A critical factor in vertical transmission of HIV+ is that the mother passes on the disease to her child. With the exception of neonatal abstinence syndrome, fetal alcohol syndrome, or genetically transmitted diseases such as Tay-Sachs Disease or Huntingtons Disease, the transmission factor is unique. A paucity of research exists in the literature on maternal attachment and genetic disorders. The minimal literature that was available on genetic transmission and psychological factors affecting the mother-child relationship was either found in theoretically based articles or was conducted in ethnically different countries.

In examining the efficacy of diagnostic genetic testing for children and adolescents at risk for Huntingtons Disease, Wertz, Fanos, & Wertz (1994) warn that parents frequently succumb to "the vulnerable child syndrome (p. 878)" and become overprotective of their children who are at risk for illness. Serban (1989) states that maternal overprotective behavior is a compensatory attempt to ward off the guilt that is experienced as a result of genetic transmission. In addition to extreme guilt, parents live "with a sense of disappointment and impending disaster (Serban, 1989, p. 200)." Denial of the disease trajectory , feelings of desperation, and unrealistic hope are other common themes that are reported by Serban. Research interviews with 36 Saudi families whose children suffered from genetically inherited disorders, concluded that mother/infant bonds were disrupted from birth.

VERTICALLY TRANSMITTED DISORDERS

Neonatal Abstinence Syndrome

Although neonatal abstinence syndrome and fetal alcohol syndrome are not genetically transmitted, they are vertically transmitted from mother to infant. Neonatal abstinence syndrome is a temporarily limited phenomenon but subjects the infant to developmental risks. Infants exposed prenatally to narcotics become addicted in utero and undergo neonatal abstinence syndrome or NAS. Neonatal abstinence syndrome is described as a central nervous system disorder characterized by hyper-irritability, gastrointestinal dysfunction, respiratory distress, and yawning, sneezing, mottling, and fever (Kaltenbach & Finnegan, 1988). The infants are not easily comforted and do not readily respond to cuddling. The findings of Kaltenbach and Finnegan indicated that the difficulty that infants with neonatal abstinence syndrome experience in visual and physical responsiveness negatively impacted attachment because the infants could not engage in reciprocal behavior with their mothers and were not easily soothed. Kaltenbach and Finnegan assert that the degree of difficulty a mother experiences in soothing her infant negatively impacts her maternal self esteem, which ultimately hinders her ability to effectively parent (Kaltenbach & Finnegan, 1988).

Fetal Alcohol Syndrome

Infants are born with fetal alcohol syndrome (FAS) as a result of alcohol consumption during a critical phase of pregnancy. Children born with fetal alcohol syndrome typically present with feeding problems, failure to thrive, and a higher susceptibility to serious illnesses during the first two years of life. Typical developmental milestones, such as motor and speech development, are often delayed. Behavior problems and hyperactivity are also more prevalent and head and body rocking, strabismus, speech and hearing impairments and inattentiveness have also been linked to FAS (Nestler & Steinhausen, 1988). Although Nestler and Steinhausen indicated that mother-infant separation was more prevalent in children with fetal alcohol syndrome (regardless of employment responsibilities), the impact on attachment of FAS is not clear. Currently, research that describes the psychological sequelae of mother-infant attachment when fetal alcohol syndrome is a factor is not available.

PREMATURE INFANTS

Preterm sick infants and mothers

When children are born to HIV+ mothers who are aware of their seropositivity, they may or may not be symptomatic at birth. However, until their seropositivity status is determined, their future is uncertain. If the child is HIV+, it is only a matter of time before the disease process will begin to impact the development and health of that child. Children who are born prematurely frequently face similar uncertain outcomes with varying degrees of postnatal illness. Mothers whose babies are born preterm and sick report (Harrison, 1983) feelings of isolation, bitterness, anger, guilt and excessive worry. They commonly experience the psychological sequelae associated with grief (Kubler-Ross, 1979; Lindemann, 1979; Rando, 1986, 1993; Raphael, 1983; Worden, 1982), which include the experience of the initial shock, denial or the inability to cognitively accept what has happened, anger, depression, bargaining, acceptance and adaptation (Harrison). Harrison reports that mothers are frequently unable to name their child until they feel fairly confident that the child will survive. The infant's inability to respond back to the mother in a reciprocal manner coupled with the mother's fear of the infant's death frequently result in delayed and/or disordered attachment (Harrison, 1983).

Fox (1988) reports that mothers of sick preterm infants treat their children with detachment, holding them farther away from their own bodies than is commonly observed with healthy infants, and overstimulating them during interaction. Like children with neonatal abstinence syndrome, sick preterm infants are less responsive and more irritable than healthy term infants. Fox observed four groups of infants who were followed from birth through age two, born mainly to Latina mothers. The groups consisted of premature infants who were healthy postnatally, premature infants who suffered respiratory distress syndrome during the postnatal period, term infants who underwent birth asphyxia postnatally, and a group of healthy term infants. Fox found that the degree of caregiver-infant interaction was strongly influenced by the infant's postnatal medical condition. It was unclear whether the mother's reactions were equally related to the infant's illness and degree of prematurity. However, it was clear that the babies who were full-term and postnatally sick received more care giving and comforting from their mothers than sick and premature infants (who were unresponsive) even though the term infants were more irritable.

The support the mothers received (i.e. gifts, visits from friends and relatives) seemed to be related to the degree of illness or prematurity (Fox, 1988). The data indicated that mothers of sick infants, whether term or premature, were less likely to receive support in the form of gifts or social support from friends and relatives. Fox hypothesized (1988) that since the giving of presents and the presence of relatives affirmed the infant as a new member of the community, the absence of these supports indicated that the infant's life was not thought of as viable or existent.

PSYCHOLOGICAL TRAUMA AND PARENTING

Parenting after Psychological Trauma

The diagnosis of HIV+ or AIDS is traumatic for mothers, who must cope with the physical and psychological sequelae with minimal support as a result of the fear of disclosure and stigma. Holocaust parents also experienced catastrophic trauma, of which they were compelled to maintain a "conspiracy of silence." Understanding the way in which Holocaust parents responded to their children may facilitate understanding of the way mothers with AIDS respond to their children.

Holocaust Survivors and Parenting

The "conspiracy of silence (Danieli, 1985)" experienced by Holocaust survivors is similar to the "conspiracy of silence" experienced by people with AIDS. Accounts of concentration camp experiences were not believed or were dismissed. Holocaust survivors were faced with the myth that they had control over their fate and could have fought against the Nazis. Moreover, they were faced with suspicions that those who had survived must have performed immoral acts. As a result, survivors felt shunned and stigmatized and refrained from relating their experiences. The resulting conspiracy of silence that existed between survivors and society impacted the survivors' familial relationships (Danieli, 1985) as survivors tended to withdraw completely into their new families. Symbiotic clinging was common as parents protected and were protected by their children. Parents were commonly depleted of all emotion and children were called on to serve as confidantes and surrogate parents (Danieli, 1985). The emotional depletion was experienced by their children as emotional detachment (Freyberg, 1980). Although emotionally depleted in terms of connectedness, survivors frequently experienced fear of recurring personal loss.

Close emotional attachments were difficult for the survivors to form when they had lost everyone and everything. Instead, they tended to regard their children as possessions meant to compensate them for what they had lost. The survivors were in deep mourning . . . This mourning was bound to be an extended, incomplete and impaired process, as it was shorn of the usual rituals . . . available for helping to work through grief and loss (Freyberg, 1980, p. 88).

ATTACHMENT

"An attachment is a reciprocal, enduring, emotional and physical affiliation between a child and a care giver (James, 1994, p. 2)." The presence of an attachment relationship is essential for a child to grow. Attachment behavior in infants and young children is action that results in maintaining the primary care giver or preferred person in proximity.. Attachment behavior is related to the emotion that accompanies it. Secure attachments result in feelings of joy and security. Threatened attachments result in feelings of jealousy, anxiety and anger and when these attachments are broken, depression and grief ensue (Bowlby, 1988). Attachment seeking behavior starts when the infant cries and these cries of discomfort cue the primary care giver to respond (James, 1994). The child seeks out the primary care giver for nurturing and comfort and receives sustenance and guidance through this relationship (Bowlby, 1973, 1982; James 1993). It is through this early attachment relationship that the child learns to self soothe, relate to others and modulate affect. A secure attachment develops when both the baby and primary care giver experience their relationship as physically and emotionally satisfying and as a source of gratification (Winnicott, 1960). The infant and young child receive sustenance and comfort and the primary care giver experiences satisfaction at the child's unfolding development (James, 1994).

The primary care giver's capacity to sensitively provide for the infant's needs are dependent on the care giver experiencing a supportive and relaxed environment herself/himself (Bowlby, 1988; Winnicott, 1960). Specific criteria impact maternal bonding and the mother's capacity to provide the necessary care taking to establish a secure attachment. These include the attitudes and expectations expressed by the mother during pregnancy about the infant and the pregnancy process itself, the birth experience, the length of time (in terms of hours or days) that the mother is separated from the baby following the birth, and the mother's early childhood experiences, traumas, and her relationship with her own parents (Bowlby, 1988). Physical or emotional unavailability of the parent or baby is a barrier to attachment. The barrier can result from physical pain, illness, developmental disability or drug addiction. Chronic emotional disturbances such as depression or extreme shame can also interfere with attachment formation (James, 1994). The essential existence of the attachment bond results in alterations of the child's behavior in order to obtain the parent's attention when the child does not receive parenting needs. Severe illness can result in impaired functioning and prolonged anxiety, which can impede the formation of or interrupt the attachment bond. When parents are needy themselves and unable to provide the emotional sustenance needed, children frequently become mini care givers themselves (James, 1994). They suppress their own needs and feelings and play an adaptive role in order to stimulate care giving in their parents (James, 1994).

The goal of attachment behavior is the maintenance of proximity and communication with the primary attachment figure and the formation of an attachment bond (Bowlby, 1980). "The formation of a bond is described as falling in love . . . (Bowlby, 1980, p. 40)."

> The child comes to perceive the care giver as the source of joy, surprise, loving warmth, and relief from pain. The care giver experiences the child's unfolding development as a source of satisfaction (James, 1944, p. 3).

Attachment and Pregnancy

During a healthy pregnancy, the mother begins to form an attachment to the child, fantasizing about what the child will be like. This attachment is crucial to the survival of the infant (Klaus & Kennell, 1982). Winnicott describes the essence of maternal care as the "primary maternal preoccupation (Winnicott, 1965, p. 87)," wherein the mother is preoccupied with the care of her baby and is able to provide almost exactly what the infant needs. Winnicott (1965) asserts that the mother must be psychologically healthy for this process to unfold.

The relationship with the developing child begins, for most women, from the time of conception or when the pregnancy is first acknowledged (Raphael, 1983). Most women experience strong emotions during pregnancy as they begin to shift their thinking from themselves to the life and well-being of their child. They commonly experience mixed feelings during the first trimester of pregnancy as they come to terms with being a mother. It is during this stage that most mothers identify the growing fetus as a part of themselves (Klaus & Kennell, 1982).

> A large number of considerations, ranging from a change in her familiar patterns to more serious matters such as economic and housing hardships or interpersonal difficulties, all influence her acceptance of the pregnancy (Klaus & Kennell, 1982, p. 12).

Psychological Reactions of Mothers to Sick Infants

Kaplan & Mason (1960) propose that the psychological reactions of mothers to sick and dying infants can be likened to acute trauma reactions and can threaten attachment. They describe this reaction as a period of disequilibrium as the mother prepares for the loss of the child. They note (Kaplan & Mason) that anticipated loss involves withdrawal from the relationship that the mother previously established prior to the birth of the child. The mother must anticipate the birth of a sick, dying child as she continues to maintain an attachment with that child. During this period of psychological turmoil, the mother must also understand, accept and perform the necessary care that is required for the sick child (Kaplan & Mason).

Most mothers experience "normal anxiety (Klaus & Kennell, 1982, p. 15)." However, any stress that leaves the mother feeling unsupported or which precipitates concern for her health or that of her child may retard or inhibit bond formation (Klaus & Kennell, 1982). Bowlby (1982) asserts that when loss of the child is threatened, anxiety and anger are likely to be aroused. Fear that the baby is sick or dying is a high risk factor that impacts bonding (Klaus & Kennell, 1982).

The infant's response to her/his mother impacts the bonding process as well. Infants who are born addicted to drugs or who are sick may fail to reach out for nourishment or for emotional contact. The failure of the infant to even minimally reach out may result in perfunctory care taking, as it impacts the mother's own bonding response (Meintz & Lynch, 1989).

Attachment and Stressful Conditions

When the attachment bond is formed and enduring, attachment behavior is only activated when stressful conditions exist such as fatigue, fear, unavailability of the primary attachment figure or strangeness (Bowlby, 1973, 1980). Adolescents and adults exhibit similar attachment behaviors when under stress (Bowlby, 1988). The greater the danger of loss of the bond (or person) the more intense and varied the actions will be in an attempt to reactivate the attachment (Bowlby, 1973, 1980). When danger of loss of the loved one exists, intense feelings and behaviors result. When parents are themselves responsible for the child's traumatic experience, they commonly react by either psychologically denying the existence of the trauma or avoiding the trauma by detaching from the child (James, 1994). Mothers with AIDS grapple with the traumatic nature of their own illness, while they commonly anticipate the loss of their seropositive child. However, the response to psychological trauma is varied and dependent on factors that will be elucidated in the following section.

PSYCHOLOGICAL TRAUMA

Theoretical Definitions of Psychological Trauma

Trauma occurs when one loses the sense of having a safe place to retreat within or outside oneself to deal with frightening emotions or experiences. This results in a state of helplessness, a feeling that one's actions have no bearing on the outcome of one's life (van der Kolk, 1987, p. 31). Since the 1970's, research has confirmed that certain stressors or traumatic events will produce difficulties in most individuals (McCann & Pearlman, 1990). The psychological literature on trauma has defined trauma as a reaction to a stressor to which most people would respond in some way (Figley, 1985; Herman, 1992; Horowitz, 1986; Lifton, 1983; Rando, 1993; & van der Kolk, 1987). Although these theorists conceptualize trauma differently, they do begin their theories with the specific stressor itself. While the aforementioned theorists account for individual response variability associated with concomitant factors and perceived situational factors, McCann and Pearlman (1990), Janoff-Bulman (1992), Higgins (1994) and Frankl (1984) focus primarily on the variability of victims' responses. These theories will be briefly described in relation to the ways in which traumatic occurrences impact human relationships and with specific reference to the psychological sequelae of living with HIV+/AIDS, if available in the literature

Stress Response Syndrome. Horowitz (1986) identified a predictable pattern of responses to serious life events which he termed the "stress response syndrome." Included in the category of serious life events are personal illness, the threat of death, dying and bereavement. Horowitz (1986) asserts that the response pattern is consistent despite individual personality differences, coping styles, or preexisting self-concepts or beliefs. Horowitz states that a stressful event contains news that causes a powerful breach in the individual's safety and violates her/his assumptive world. Following the event, individuals respond initially with an outcry that is accompanied with strong emotions such as fear, sadness or rage. The initial outcry may be initially delayed as the individual copes with the situation at hand but is ultimately evidenced when the trauma is confronted. Horowitz states that the response symptoms to a stressful life event are initially most commonly expressed by denial and then by an oscillation between denial and numbing or intrusive repetitious thoughts and emotions of the trauma. During the phase of denial, the individual tries to avoid the traumatic event. The person commonly ignores the implications of the threat or loss, cognitively denies the reality of the situation, and may exhibit withdrawal of interest in life and emotional and behavioral constriction. These symptoms function to reestablish psychological equilibrium. Intrusive images, emotions, thoughts and physical feelings form the other reactive phase to trauma. During this phase, the individual commonly experiences shame, rage, and fear. The oscillation between denial and intrusion continues until the individual has worked through the process and has integrated the event in her/his life (Horowitz, 1986). The working through process is complete when the pre-event mental representations, self-images and behaviors are changed in addition to the intrapsychic integration of the event itself (Horowitz).

Overwhelming threat. Figley (1985) defines psychic trauma as an immediate situation that confronts the individual with an overwhelming threat. Figley differentiates traumatic responses to natural catastrophes and to those catastrophes that could be avoided. According to this theory, the events that could be avoided are more emotionally troublesome and more difficult to resolve. Figley further differentiates those who remain victimized by the event and those who "overcome (Figley, p. 400)" the catastrophe. He asserts that

> Victims and survivors are similar in that they both experienced a traumatic event. But while the victim has been immobilized and discouraged by the event, the survivor has overcome the traumatic memories and become mobile. The survivor draws on experiences of coping with the catastrophe as a source of strength , while the victim remains immobilized (Figley, 1985, p. 399).

However, Figley maintains that characterological differences and cognitive processes, which include personal life theories, account for differentiation among trauma responses within the aforementioned categories. Figley asserts that "individual differences, . . . characteristics of the catastrophe, and initial reactions to the catastrophe," determine reactions to catastrophes. He further maintains that the individual's initial response (within six-21 days) to the trauma is predictive of posttraumatic problems. Figley maintains that the role of the family is crucial for the individual recovering from traumatic experiences. One way in which the family can facilitate recovery is by serving as a "sounding board (Figley, p. 409)" and by "offering or supporting new . . . perspective on the catastrophe (Figley, p. 409)."

Posttraumatic Stress Syndrome. Herman (1992) asserts that when the exposure to trauma is severe, no person is immune to the traumatic response of posttraumatic stress disorder (Herman, 1992). Although the specific type of trauma, the availability of support, and other individual variables influence the adaptation to the specific trauma, the core features of posttraumatic syndrome are fairly consistent. People who are already detached from others or who feel disempowered are the most at risk for the posttraumatic syndrome (Herman, 1992). Herman asserts that the experience of trauma has its greatest impact on interpersonal attachments. "Trauma impels people both to withdraw from close relationships and to seek them desperately (Herman, 1992, p. 56)." When the individual has experienced trauma, intimate relationships are compromised by the contradictory feelings of intense need and also intense fear of another violation of the attachment bond. When feelings of helplessness and victimization persist, people who experience continuous trauma may lose the feeling that they have any control over what happens to them. When feelings of helplessness and terror persist, such as is commonly experienced when diagnosed with a life-threatening illness, the need for attachment and protection dramatically increase. This sense of helplessness and neediness often makes it difficult to modulate the degree of intimate involvement with others and frequently results in relationships that fluctuate between extremes (Herman, 1992; van der Kolk, 1987). Traumatized people feel abandoned and disconnected from even their closest relationships yet are able to mobilize their protective capacities to care for their children (Herman, 1992).

Human response to overwhelming events. The ". . . human response to overwhelming and uncontrollable life events is remarkably consistent (van der Kolk, 1987, p. 2)." At the core of the psychological response to trauma is the oscillation between reliving and denial or the alternation between intrusive and numbing responses (van der Kolk). During the intrusive phase, the person who has been traumatized is psychologically or physiologically aroused. When aroused, the individual responds with either explosive aggressive outbursts directed against the self or others or with social and emotional withdrawal. The numbing response consists of emotional constriction, social isolation and a sense of estrangement. Irritability and loss of the ability to modulate anger are central to the trauma response. In order to gain control over the trauma response, people who have experienced trauma frequently avoid all situations or emotions that are related to the trauma.

Death imprint. Lifton (1980) explains a traumatic event as one that threatens the survival of the individual. He describes the "death imprint" as the key to the survivor's experience. "The death imprint consists of the radical intrusion of an image-feeling of threat or end to life (Lifton, p. 169)." The intrusion of death may be sudden or gradual. The death imprint includes fear of dying and anxiety associated with the disintegration of the self. When faced with this threat, the individual experiences limited capacity with which to respond. Simultaneously, the survivor experiences survival guilt if she/he has survived and others have died.

> . . . every death encounter is itself a reactivation of earlier 'survivals.' The degree of anxiety associated with the death imprint has to do with the impossibility of assimilating the death imprint-because of its suddenness, its extreme or protracted nature, or its association with the terror of premature, unacceptable dying (Lifton, 1980, p. 169).

Lifton states that during acute grief, when confronted with loss, adults react with a depressive position that is a combination of "constricted sadness and suppressed rage (Lifton, p. 188)." When experiencing acute grief, interpersonal relationships can be characterized by extreme touchiness, constriction, anger and pain.

Will to Live

Viktor Frankl (1984) proposed that an individual can cope with the acute grief and death anxiety that Lifton described by developing a meaning or "why to live (Frankl, 1984, p. 97)." For Frankl, this meaning is unique to each individual and is the primary motivator of life. The meaning for a person who is grappling with life threatening illness can be the opportunity that the individual takes in the way that she/he copes with her burden of suffering. Frankl described Nazi concentration camp existence where the individual was constantly faced with death and with unspeakable atrocities. In answer to his quest to determine why some survived this experience and why others died of depression, he explained that "Life ultimately means taking the responsibility to find the right answer to its problems and to fulfill the tasks which it constantly sets for each individual (Frankl, 1984, p. 98)."

Cognitive Schemas

Janoff-Bulman (1992) explains that basic views of the world and the self represent the individual's orientation towards the "total push and pull of the cosmos (Janoff-Bulman, 1992, p. 4)." These schemas are patterns around which experience is organized and perceived. She proposes that over time, an individual develops a conceptual system that provides her/him with expectations about the world and about herself/himself. These assumptions are hierarchically based, abstract, and pervasive. Whether an event is perceived as traumatic or not is particular to the individual involved and the way in which the event is understood.

> Those events that seem most overwhelming do not produce a traumatic response in every survivor, and other life events that may not be considered very threatening may, in fact, produce a traumatic response in some survivors (Janoff-Bulman, 1992, p. 52).

Janoff-Bulman states that the individual perceives an experience as being traumatic when it violates her/his fundamental assumptions about the world. "The injury is to the victim's inner world. Core assumptions are shattered by the traumatic experience (Janoff-Bulman, 1992, p. 52)."

Rando (1993) describes the "assumptive world" as a construction by which the individual interprets incoming data and orients herself/himself. "In large part, the assumptive world determines the individual's needs, emotions and behavior, and gives rise to hopes, wishes, fantasies and dreams (Rando, 1993, p. 50)." Rando states that the ability to revise the assumptive world, when it has been traumatically violated, depends on the centrality and meaning of the assumption, and the number of primary and concurrent losses with which the individual must cope. Rando states that a traumatic event is more shattering when the old assumptions have been tenaciously held.

Rando maintains (1993) that victims experience "secondary victimization" or additional traumatization when they are "blamed" for their own victimization. Secondary victimization results when others, who are not effected, try to maintain their own assumptive world by isolating and stigmatizing the individuals who have experienced the trauma. Rando (1993) describes AIDS as the

> ... archetypal dread disease because it contains all the worst elements of the great pandemics ... , which devastated entire communities, and the shameful stigmas (e.g., cancer and leprosy), associated with an insidious and painful process of individual death (p. 632).

She asserts that people with AIDS and those who have survived the death of a loved one from AIDS-related illness are at significant risk for complicated mourning because of the factors that are associated with this illness, which are lengthy illness, preventability, and lack of social support. The two issues that are especially salient to AIDS-related illnesses and deaths are stigmatization and disenfranchisement. These two issues complicate the stress response syndrome, can complicate the mourning process and exacerbate trauma reactions (Rando, 1993).

Resilience

McCann and Pearlman (1990) assert that an experience is traumatic when an individual perceives it to be so and that it is important to avoid grouping individuals as trauma "survivors" with the assumption that they all experience the same set of responses. They define trauma as the individual's psychological response—not as the stressor itself. An experience becomes traumatic when it threatens the psychological core of the individual. "Thus, one person's trauma may be another person's difficult experience (McCann & Pearlman, 1990, p. 12)." The events that surround a trauma, the meaning of these events to the survivor and the support, or lack of support, by others contribute to the survivor's reactions. McCann and Pearlman assert that the psychological reaction of the survivor is an integration of self capacities, ego resources, cognitive schemas and psychological needs. Schemas, or the cognitive manifestation of psychological needs, develop in relation to oneself and others. Over time schemas, and concomitant feelings and thoughts, become unique to the individual. Schemas can be disrupted by life experiences that are discrepant to them. In the ordinary course of life, new information about the self and world is assimilated into existing schemas.

> When a situation occurs that cannot be 'fit' into existing schemas, an accommodation or change in schemas occurs. If the discrepancy between one's existing schemas and life experiences is extreme and perceived as threatening, the event is psychologically shocking. If this discrepancy occurs within a need area that is central to the individual, the event will be experienced as traumatic (McCann & Pearlman, 1990, p. 59).

Higgins (1994) describes individuals who, although having experienced what she would describe as traumatic events, were able to overcome their past and flourish. She described these individuals as being resilient. These individuals believe that the best commingles with the worst—that goodness exists and that they are worthy of love. They make a conscious decision not to be subordinated to their suffering. She further explains the significance that interpretation of experiences has for the resilient. They find goodness in difficult situations while maintaining faith in human relationships. Higgins states that ". . . faith is the activity of meaning-making in its most ultimate and intimate dimensions—finding pattern, order, and significance to our lives (Higgins, 1994, p. 172)." This faith can be described as "convictional knowing" through which individuals invest their "hearts" (Higgins, p. 173)" as anchors to ground their lives. This faith can be strong religious or moral convictions that individuals perceive as greater than themselves.

McCann and Pearlman (1990) state that "The diagnosis of any terminal illness disrupts one's schemas related to safety and invulnerability (p. 305)." In addition to facing premature death and physical decline that are common to any chronic serious illness, people with AIDS must also face the uncertainty of ultimate death and/or chronic illness. They assert that people who are HIV+ are victims of psychological trauma and are at risk for posttraumatic stress disorder (McCann & Pearlman). Negative esteem schemas develop as a result of the contagion, stigma and social rejection associated with AIDS. Decreased ability to care for oneself and disrupted schemas for intimacy, that can result from fear of being contagious as well as the social isolation that is associated with AIDS, contribute to and exacerbate negative esteem schemas and therefore, psychological trauma (McCann & Pearlman, 1990).

Studies Citing AIDS-Related Trauma and Psychological Sequelae

Martin (1988) interviewed 745 gay men in New York City to determine the relationship between AIDS-related bereavement and psychological stress. Findings indicated that symptoms of distress increased directly with the number of bereavements (lover or close friend) experienced. The results of the study predicted serious psychological distress following the deaths of one or more close friends or a lover due to AIDS.

Other Trauma-Related Studies

Davidson and Baum (1986) studied the relationship between chronic stress and symptoms of posttraumatic stress disorder in people living within 5 miles of the Three Mile Island nuclear power station. Five years following the incident, mothers living near the damaged reactor continued to experience increased anxiety and depression, to report greater symptoms of distress, to exhibit greater emotional arousal and to perform more poorly on stress-sensitive tasks, when compared with mothers who lived near an undamaged nuclear power station. Although deaths did not occur as a direct result of Three Mile Island, the perceived threat of radiation exposure and concomitant medical consequences remained. Thus, living with perceived threat continued to result in exacerbated psychological symptoms, that are similar to those experienced by women with AIDS, who contend with varying levels of death anxiety, even when symptomatology is diminished.

GRIEF AND MOURNING

Bereavement

Women with AIDS have been diagnosed with a life threatening illness, for which there is currently no cure. Reactions of grief and loss commonly accompany the diagnosis and anticipated loss of life. Bereavement is the reaction to the loss of a close relationship or to the potential loss of one's own life. Mourning is the process of undoing the psychological bonds that bound or attached the bereaved to the deceased (Raphael, 1983) and the psychological process that ensues after a fatal diagnosis or during a terminal illness (Rando, 1986; Lindemann, 1979). A syndrome of psychological, physiological and interpersonal reactions ensues that includes heightened preoccupation with the deceased or with the self and painful feelings of sorrow, loss of appetite and excessive fatigue, and excessive feelings of helplessness, hostility and the inability to interact successfully (Lindemann, 1979). The bereavement reaction is a series of phases that represent the process of adaptation to loss. These phases are not fixed or linear (Parkes & Weiss, 1983; Rando, 1993; Raphael, 1983).

Rando (1993) describes the three phases of bereavement that include concomitant processes and emotional and cognitive responses. She has described these phases as avoidance, confrontation and accommodation. The Avoidance Phase covers the period of time in which the news of the death, or other loss, is initially received and a short period of time thereafter. This period of time is marked by the desire to avoid acknowledgement of the death or loss. "Like the physical shock that occurs with trauma to the body, the human psyche goes into shock with the traumatic assault of the death of the loved one (Rando, 1993, p. 33)." As recognition of the loss becomes clearer, denial immediately sets in and serves as a buffer, allowing the individual to gradually absorb reality. Denial is a defensive mechanism that enables the individual to negate, or push out of consciousness, painful or intolerable thoughts. The processes required to move through the Avoidance Phase are acknowledgement of the death or loss and an understanding of what has happened (Rando, 1993; Raphael, 1982).

During the Confrontation Phase, grief and the reactions to the loss are experienced most acutely. "Separation from the loved one generates alarm in the mourner, which results in heightened autonomic arousal, anger, and protest, and calls forth biologically based searching behavior (Rando, 1993, p. 34)." The mourner reacts to the urge to recover and reunite with the loved one (Bowlby, 1980, Parkes & Weiss, 1983). Lifton (1983) and Rando (1993) assert that the dying person confronts death by attacking and directing this anger inwards in the form of depression or outwards in angry outbursts towards people and/or things. In order to move through the Confrontation Phase, the bereaved must react to the loss, review and remember the lost relationship, and relinquish the attachment to the deceased in the way in which the bereaved has known this tie to be (Rando, 1993).

The final phase in this paradigm is the Accommodation Phase where the bereaved experiences a decline in the symptoms of acute grief and begins to reenter the everyday world with the establishment of a new identity and a changed assumption about self and the world. Although theorists (Kubler-Ross, 1969; Lindemann, 1979; Worden, 1982) have described this phase as resolution, or the assumption of a final closure between the deceased and the bereaved, Rando (1986, 1993) asserts that the loss must be integrated into the rest of life and that final closure only occurs at the time of the bereaved's death. For Rando (1986, 1993), the process inherent in the Accommodation Phase is to reinvest in the new world without forgetting the old.

Bowlby (1980) divides bereavement into four phases. Initially the bereaved or dying person feels numbed and unable to process the information. Intense anxiety and the yearning to search for and recover the lost person characterize this phase. A period of disorganization and despair follow during which time strong emotions are experienced as the bereaved asks endless questions about how and why of the loss. The self is redefined during the final stage, or reorganization, in this theory. Bowlby describes this final phase as a process of "reshaping internal representational models so as to align them with the changes that have occurred in the bereaved's life situation (Bowlby, 1980, p. 94)."

Complicated Mourning

Complicated mourning occurs when there is a distortion or failure to work through some phase of the mourning process (Lindemann, 1944; Sanders, 1989; Rando, 1993). Symptoms of chronic mourning can include chronic anger, irritability and depression, self-destructive behaviors (including the initiation or exacerbation of substance abuse), the chronic experience of numbness, alienation and depersonalization, fear of intimacy, heightened death anxiety, and psychological and behavioral restlessness (Lindemann, 1944; Sanders, 1989; Rando, 1993; Parkes, 1988). Variables that have been associated with complicated mourning (that are germane to this study) are death from an overly long illness, death of a child, serial losses that are not worked through, lack of social support, and concurrent mourner stresses and health problems (Lindemann, 1944; Rando, 1993; Worden, 1992).

Diagnosis of a Life-Threatening Illness

The individual diagnosed with a life-threatening illness will likely react as she/he would to any major trauma (Doka, 1993) and will likely begin a mourning process. Important variables that impact the dying person's reactions to this traumatic situation are her/his personality, mental health, lifestyle, coping ability, economic status, and access to quality medical treatment. The effects of physical and mental deterioration, the treatment regime, available support and the type of social reaction to the illness contribute to the dying person's reactions. Shorter survival times are reported in individuals who indicate having poor social relationships (Rando, 1984). These individuals are more likely to utilize denial and repression as coping mechanisms (Rando, 1984, 1993). Rando (1993) asserts that psychic numbing is at the heart of the trauma reaction to death. Lifton (1983) states that when the individual experiences psychic numbing, she/he is unable to feel compassion for others because the self is severed from any feeling.

> In a personal encounter with death, the individual experiences helplessness, anxiety, heightened arousal, fear, terror, a sense of abandonment, increased vulnerability, and the yearning for relief and

rescue. The traumatic stimulus of such an event can overwhelm the
ego and cause post-traumatic stress reactions (Rando, 1993, p. 587).

As the dying individual experiences post-traumatic stress reactions,
she/he commonly experiences reduced emotional responsiveness and
exhibits less interest and involvement in interpersonal relationships
(Figley, 1985).

Psychological Processes Inherent in a Life-Threatening Illness

The tasks of the grief process associated with severe chronic illness are
to accept the reality of the inherent physical losses and potential loss of
life, to experience and resolve grief emotions, to reinvest emotional
energy to other things, or to reassess or rebuild spiritual meaning and
faith (Doka, 1990). Doka (1993) characterizes the time of diagnosis as a
time of crisis where the individual characteristically responds with
inward attention and egocentricity. The crisis recedes during the
chronic phase of the illness and is characterized by preoccupation with
self, heightened awareness of the body and fear that physical symptoms
or reactions may indicate relapse, metastasis, or reoccurrence (Doka,
1993). The period of time after the diagnosis has been called the
"living-dying interval (Rando, 1986, p. 5)," a period of extreme and
repetitive stress. The psychological coping mechanisms utilized to deal
with this stress are related to the phase of acceptance of the illness and
the degree of symptomatology present (Rando, 1986).

> In the initial acute phase there are likely to be transient maladaptive
> coping mechanisms. In the chronic living-dying interval coping
> mechanisms normal to the developmental stage of the patient can be
> expected. In the terminal phase, typical coping mechanisms recede
> and tend to be replaced by isolating mechanisms . . . (Rando, 1984, p.
> 252).

In the living-dying interval, terminally ill people vacillate between
death acceptance and denial (Doka, 1993; Rando, 1984, 1993). The
dying person can cope with the threat of extinction by retreating, by

excluding the threat of death from awareness or by mastering the situation. By regressing, the individual becomes egocentric and dependent. Repressed and suppressed death awareness results in the attempt to exclude intolerable thoughts of death from consciousness, either unconsciously or consciously. Faced with the extreme stress of the terminal diagnosis, the dying person commonly represses all thoughts of the condition into the unconscious. This mechanism is only useful on a limited basis since symptoms are a constant reminder of the illness. In contrast to repression, suppression is a conscious attempt to exclude thoughts of death from awareness. Denial is a coping mechanism whereby the diagnosed individual negates or pushes out of consciousness painful or intolerable thoughts.

Rando (1984) has differentiated between first, second and third order psychological denial. First order denial usually occurs in the prediagnostic phase when the individual denies the existence of specific facts of the illness. In order for the individual to admit the diagnosis, disease symptoms must be present. In second order denial, the individual admits the presence of symptoms and the diagnosis itself, but refuses to admit to the implications of the disease process. In third order denial, the individual recognizes that the disease is incurable but denies the possibility of death (Rando, 1984).

Sarwer and Crawford (1994) assert that people with AIDS respond to their illness and the disease trajectory by following coping stages that mirror Kubler-Ross's (1969) stages of mourning. These stages that detail the emotional course that many people with AIDS experience are denial, anger, bargaining, depression and acceptance. Sarwer and Crawford also delineate three stages of denial, the first stage being characterized by lack of affect as the person who is sick discusses her/his illness. When experiencing second order denial, the person with AIDS would be less likely to discuss her/his illness. Third order denial is described as high risk behavior that does not benefit the individual. In this paradigm, the second stage of intrapsychic integration of the illness involves anger, which can commonly be directed towards friends and family of the person with AIDS. Sarwer and Crawford report that anger is the first emotion experienced by people when they experience their first AIDS-related illness, although anger can erupt even when the person is asymptomatic. The third stage in this model is bargaining and involves offers of personal sacrifice in exchange for health or longevity. They assert that bargaining is driven by guilt; when bargaining fails, depression is commonly experienced. Acceptance of the self and of the terminal illness occurs during the final stage of this model.

When confronting anxiety about one's impending death, the dying person frequently closes off all feelings and experiences inner deadness (Rando, 1993). Both Lifton (1983) and Rando (1993) maintain that the individual confronts death anxiety by attacking. Rando asserts that ". . . it appears the survivor is more comfortable dealing with anger than with guilt or other forms of severe anxiety (1993, p. 585)."

Secondary Losses Associated with Life-Threatening Illness

Diagnosis of and living with a life threatening and debilitating illness presents a combination of problems to the afflicted individual. In addition to concerns about job loss, financial security and health costs, the individual commonly grapples with the illness itself. As the individual faces the terminal illness, fears of disfigurement and debilitation frequently accompany the factors associated with death anxiety. The dying person can become increasingly isolated as family and friends try to avoid witnessing the illness. She/he mourns for lost relationships, for loss of herself/himself, for loss of the present and future, and for loss of intimacy. "This loneliness appears to be most paramount when individuals face the prospect of death and dread that they will be deserted in dying (Rando, 1984, p. 234)."

Anticipatory Grief

During the living-dying interval a number of problems originate as a result of the chronic nature of terminal illness. These include numerous remissions and relapses exacerbated by periods of uncertainty, each associated with numerous psychological reactions. As the loved ones witness and react to the gradual decline of the dying person and to the treatment regimes that are associated with the terminal illness, they begin to anticipate the death. Rando (1986) defines anticipatory grief as an adaptational response to impending death wherein the bereaved prepares for life without the person who is dying, detaching from present and future hopes. The process of detachment and readjustment to the environment in which the loved one will no longer be present can be beneficial to the bereaved because it can prepare the bereaved for the mourning after the death. As the bereaved psychologically prepares for this life change, emotional decathexis can occur. The conflicting demands of the living-dying period are the simultaneous processes of letting go of the dying person's future image intrapsychically while drawing closer to the dying person, as increased attention, energy and behaviors are needed in the present. However, Rando's research indicates that continued involvement with the dying individual can become altered when the living-dying interval is longer than eighteen months (Rando, 1986). The long-term anticipation of the loss coupled with the increased care that is frequently needed can result in emotional and physical exhaustion and even relief after the death.

Parkes and Weiss (1983) dispute the idea that anticipation of the loss can result in premature detachment. "Only in exceptional circumstances do people become detached from a dying person (Parkes & Weiss, 1983, p. 58)." Conversely, they propose that anticipation of the loss serves to intensify the attachment. In fact, Parkes and Weiss assert that separation anxiety occurs as a result of emotional reaction to the threat of loss. They define separation anxiety as the ". . . expression of the urge to stay close to or search for a person to whom an individual is attached (Parkes & Weiss, p. 58)." Their observations indicate that individuals informed of the death of a loved one were initially unable to grasp the full implications of the information. They experienced deep intense grief as they came to accept the reality of the impending loss. "There was, in many cases, a stubborn persistence of this grieving, as though it would not be relinquished (Parkes & Weiss, p. 57)." The separation anxiety diminished after the actual loss and was replaced with a period of conscious relinquishing and despair (Parkes, & Weiss). Regardless of how long the period of forewarning is, detachment or "giving up" does not occur until after the death (Parkes & Weiss).

Anticipatory grief taxes the psychological resources of the dying person because it poses a problem that is not solvable and therefore stimulates a crisis period characterized by mounting tension (Rando, 1986). During this period, feelings of anger, which may be directed at family and friends, and depression are common and expectable, as more regressed coping mechanisms are utilized (Bowlby, 1973. 1980; Doka,

1993). Although the dying person may deny her/his anticipated death, losses that are inherent in terminal illness cannot be denied. These losses include loss of functioning, body parts, relationships, future hopes and dreams, predictability and control (Rando, 1986). In addition to intrapsychically integrating these losses while in a state of heightened anxiety, the dying person must frequently attend to medical care needs, psychosocial problems that are engendered by the diagnosis, and future plans for survivors. Once the diagnosis and prognosis are accepted, the dying person may experience deep despair (Doka, 1993). During the terminal phase of dying, the dying person typically replaces coping mechanisms with withdrawal and increased detachment (Kubler-Ross, 1969; Doka, 1993).

Parental Loss of a Child

> All the deaths of childhood are abhorrent and so especially stressful. Furthermore, there is societal expectation that children should not die. Parents are likely to feel that they somehow failed, that society will condemn them when death does occur (Raphael, 1983, p. 235).

Rando (1986) reports that parental loss of a child is experienced more severely than any other death. Bereaved parents are more likely to experience intensified guilt, anger, pain on separation, yearning, despair, violations of their assumptive world and upsurges of acute grief. "The simple fact is that what is considered abnormal or pathological in other losses is typical after the death of a child . . . (Rando, 1993, p. 630)." Raphael (1983) reports that an exacerbating factor in parental loss of a child is the untimeliness of the death. In most developed countries, parents expect that children will live to reach adult life and survive their own parents. This assumption is violated by the child's fatal illness. Progressive, debilitating and malignant diseases are particularly painful for parents to witness as their child's body is taken over by disease process. Diseases with congenital etiology are particularly burdensome and carry with them added parental shame and guilt (Raphael, 1983).

Disenfranchised Grief

Disenfranchised grief is response to loss that cannot be openly acknowledged, publicly mourned or socially supported (Doka, 1989). The grief may not be supported or acknowledged, in the case of a diagnosis of HIV+ or AIDS, due to the social stigma, isolation and rejection that accompanies this disease. The lack of social support during the periods of diagnosis, chronic illness, and death can result in intensified and complicated grief (Doka, 1989).

Mothers, Children, and AIDS

In addition to the commonly experienced concerns and stressors for the individual diagnosed with HIV+ or AIDS, the diagnosis of a mother and her child present additional stressors. The mother's psychological response to her own diagnosis will be impacted by whether the diagnosis is determined prior to pregnancy, during pregnancy or as a result of the child's symptoms and subsequent diagnosis (James, 1988). The way in which the mother responds to her infant and to the infant's terminal diagnosis will be influenced by her psychological reaction to her own terminal illness and the way in which she psychologically integrates this trauma. The manner in which the trauma is psychologically integrated is influenced by the degree of experienced symptoms, by the dangers already present in the individual's life (Levine & Dubler, 1990), and by the characteristic response pattern of the individual to crisis (Doka, 1993). The presence or absence of disease symptoms will likely influence the intrapsychic integration of the diagnosis and prognosis.

SUMMARY OF LITERATURE REVIEW

The majority of women with AIDS in the United States are currently African American or Latina, comprising 75% of the women with AIDS. Most of these women live in urban areas, where they must contend with violence and poverty on a daily basis. Women are the fastest growing group of People With AIDS; the disease is spreading in other ethnic groups and in areas that are not predominantly poor as well.

The diagnosis of a life-threatening illness, such as HIV+/AIDS, has been shown to be traumatic and is associated with psychological sequelae that include death anxiety, irritability and anger, suicidality and depression. As is the case with other life-threatening illnesses such as cancer, the person with the disease commonly responds to the disease trajectory with psychological sequelae of grief.

The physical manifestations of HIV+/AIDS vary. However, for uncertain reasons, the disease process in women progresses at a faster rate than that of men. AIDS-related exhaustion and the opportunistic infections that erupt as the immune system deteriorates, impede the ability of affected individuals to adequately care for themselves.

Studies in the literature elucidated the traumatizing and exhausting consequences of caring for a child with AIDS. Many of the parents who were interviewed reported experiencing feelings of anger, shame and depression. The anticipated loss of a child has been described as the most painful loss to bear. Controversial theories in the literature indicate that either increased attachment or decathexis result when parents anticipate the death of their child. Mothers, who are themselves often extremely ill as a result of AIDS-related conditions, must care for their child with vertically transmitted AIDS, who is frequently neurologically impaired and developmentally delayed. The minimal research that has been done in this area indicated that mothers with AIDS experienced intensified attachments to their children with AIDS, and that their children gave meaning to their lives.

The literature review has shown that people who are coping with their own catastrophic illness experience heightened emotions and increased need for emotional support. Concomitantly, parents who are caring for children with devastating illnesses, such as pediatric AIDS, experience similar emotions and needs. As a result of fear of disclosure and societal stigma, mothers with AIDS frequently care for their children with AIDS in isolation, and turn to their seronegative children for emotional support.

III

Methodology

QUALITATIVE RESEARCH

This study used a qualitative research design to acquire the stories of women who have vertically transmitted HIV+ or AIDS to their children and the stories of women who live with the potential for transmission. Questions were formulated to ascertain both the psychological impact of the HIV+ infection on emotional sequelae and on mother-child relationships. Qualitative data consist of direct quotations from people about their experiences, beliefs, feelings and attitudes as well as detailed descriptions of observed behaviors and case histories. The data are collected as open-ended narratives in the natural settings of the participants. The researcher using the qualitative approach attempts to capture what people have to say in their own words (Berg, 1980).

> The purpose of gathering responses to open-ended questions is to enable the researcher to understand and capture the points of view of other people without predetermining those points of view through prior selection of questionnaire categories (Berg, p. 28).

An advantage of qualitative research is that the measures used allow the researcher to record and understand people in their own terms. It provides a synthesized description of people's self-reports of their internal states, that is not possible using a quantitative design. In qualitative research, the questions are open-ended in order to understand the meanings that people have ascribed to their lives and experiences (Berg, 1980).

Phenomenological Methodology

Using the phenomenological approach, the researcher attempts to understand the conscious meaning that the participant reveals in her/his narrative (Seidman, 1991). The investigator most commonly seeks to understand perceptions and feelings of people through in-depth, intensive interviewing. When using the phenomenological approach, the perceptions of those interviewed become subjective study findings . The researcher initially uses an inductive approach in the interview process until emerging patterns are revealed in the inquiry. As these patterns appear, the researcher focuses on these emerging patterns in a more deductive approach. Seidman (1991) suggests interviewing research participants on more than one occasion in order to explore the context of their lives and experiences.

Selection of Participants

Pediatric HIV programs, physicians who specialize in infectious disease, and service programs for people with AIDS were contacted in order to locate study participants. Criteria for study participation were that the woman have HIV+ or AIDS, that the potential for vertical transmission existed with at least one of her children, and that she had taken care of this child at least some of the time since birth. Thirteen women with HIV+ or AIDS were interviewed for this study. Five of the women had vertically transmitted AIDS to their child/children. Four of the women were uncertain of their childrens' disease status at the time of the interviews because of the diagnostic procedures used at the pediatric HIV+ programs at which their children were monitored. The possibility for vertical transmission was non-existent with one of the woman because the virus was transmitted to her many years after the birth of her children. However, she felt that being a mother with AIDS had influenced her relationship with her children. She requested to participate in the study because it was important to her that her story be told.

Twelve of the participants were connected with specialized programs for people with AIDS that have psychotherapy, case management and social service components available. Two of the participants were associated with a pediatric HIV program in a New England medical center. One of the participants learned of the study from her physician who is the Director of Infectious Diseases in another New England medical center. Eight of the study participants were associated with an HIV consortium in southern New England that offers free services such as case management, support groups, transportation and child care assistance, home delivered meals, medications and financial assistance to people with HIV+. Two of the women interviewed participate in an AIDS support group associated with the Visiting Nurses Association in a New England city. They learned about the research when written information about the study was given to the members by the group facilitator. Written information about the research project was posted, with stamped reply cards, at two other programs in New England that offer services for people with AIDS. Responses were not received from people associated with either of these programs.

STUDY METHOD

The Internal Review Board associated with the Department of Clinical Psychology at Antioch New England Graduate School approved the research methodology before potential sites were contacted. Prior to conducting the research in this study, staff at the programs that facilitated participant selection evaluated and approved the intent, objectives, and methodology of this study by reviewing a research proposal. In addition, interviews with administrators and medical staff took place at two of the sites.

After the study was approved, the directors of the Pediatric HIV Program in a New England medical center, sent a letter endorsing the research to thirteen potential participants. Included with the letter were forms to be completed if the woman was interested in study participation and stamped self-addressed envelopes. Telephone numbers were requested so that this researcher could personally contact the potential participants. Two women from this program indicated interest in participating in the research and were initially contacted by telephone. During the telephone contact, the intent and methodology of the study were explained. Both of these women agreed to participate and were interviewed in their homes on two separate occasions. One of the women was contacted in a follow-up telephone call. Telephone follow-up was not possible with the second participant whose telephone number had been changed to an unlisted number.

The study was approved after a personal interview with the director of the HIV consortium and one of the case managers where the study proposal and methodology were presented along with written documentation. Following this meeting, case managers explained the study and participation requirements to all of their clients who fit the study criteria. Eight women agreed to participate in the research. Six of the participants were brought to one of the program offices, by their case manager, where the interviews took place. Two of the participants were interviewed in their homes. Four of the women were interviewed with an interpreter because their primary language was Spanish. The other four women were bilingual and communicated in English during the interview process. In order to ensure accuracy in the transcribed data, an independent Spanish speaking interpreter reviewed the audiotapes and found the interviews to be accurately transcribed.

After reading the research proposal, the Director of Infectious Diseases in another New England medical center contacted three women with whom he was working and described the research study to them. They were provided with a way to contact this researcher by telephone if interested in study participation. Two women indicated interest. Only one of these women met the study participation criteria and she was interviewed in this researcher's office on two separate occasions.

Initial contact was made with a member of the AIDS team connected with the Visiting Nurses Association in another large New England city. Written information describing the study was requested. The facilitator of a support group for women with AIDS, run by the VNA, distributed a description of the study intent, methodology, and selection criteria to members of this group. Two women contacted this researcher by telephone indicating their interest in participation. They were each individually interviewed one time in their homes.

The original study design consisted of an initial interview, lasting about 1 1/2 hours, a second interview which was a fifteen minute check-in and a follow-up telephone contact. All interviews were audiotaped and transcribed verbatim. The identity of each participant was kept confidential and numbers were used to identify the transcribed narratives. The audiotapes and transcriptions were kept in a locked file cabinet to ensure confidentiality. A copy of the audiotape was offered to each participant at the completion of the interview process. One of the participants requested the audiotape and stated that she would leave the tape for her two sons after her death so that they would know of her love for them and of the feelings that she had not previously expressed to anyone else. The other audiotapes were destroyed.

Although the research design called for interviewing each participant two times within one to two weeks, changes due to the disease process, personal problems, other medical appointments, and other medical issues were accommodated. Six of the participants agreed to the second interview. However, five of the participants reported that they were either too ill or that their lives were too complicated to participate in a second interview. One of the participants was unable to participate in a second interview due to the birth of her child several days following the initial interview. Lack of personal safety at the home of one of the participants led to the decision to only conduct a single interview.

The original research design included a $25.00 stipend to be given at the end of the second interview. Compensation in the form of a $25.00 stipend was given to the participants at the end of the first interview because only half of the women indicated the interest, need, or ability to participate in the second interview. In addition, several of the women requested that they be given the money at the initial interview due to severe financial constraints. At the initial interview, the participants were informed that they had the right to withdraw from the study at any time during the interview process. Each participant was informed of the risks and benefits of involvement in the study verbally and in a Consent Form that they were asked to sign. The Consent Form follows the federal regulations on the protection of human participants (Federal Regulations, Title 45, Part 46, 1991). A copy of the Consent Form can be found in the Appendix.

Follow-up telephone calls were made to eleven of the participants one to three weeks following the final interview to assess for any emotional exacerbation as a result of the research participation. This researcher was unable to locate two of the women because one woman had changed her telephone number to an unlisted number, and the other woman had moved out of the area. All the women indicated, either at the personal interview or by the follow-up telephone call, that they had benefited from participating in the study. They stated that having the opportunity to express their feelings regarding their seropositivity and their concern for and relationship with their children was very important to them because they had not been afforded this opportunity previously. They reported that they were either not asked about their feelings and emotions by other service providers because their relationship was more task oriented, or that they were not comfortable expressing these feelings with the professionals. In addition, many of the women stated that they themselves had not been in touch with their feelings prior to their participation in the study. Many of the women cried during the interviews and they all reported that their emotional expressions felt cathartic.

The study utilized an open-ended interview to access the unique experience of each participant. The interviews began with questions regarding demographics and background information. These questions included: name, DOB, age, race, ethnicity, children, HIV+ status of self and child/children, symptoms present in self and child, help with children, living arrangements, relational status, sexual orientation, drug use, pregnancy status, when and how learned of HIV+ status, medication used, present HIV+ status, current symptoms, hospitalizations, medical problems, and losses by death.

RESEARCH QUESTIONS SPECIFICALLY FORMULATED FOR THE STUDY

1. How do you remember feeling when you were given the information that you were HIV+?

2. How did you decide to carry your pregnancy to term (if seropositive status was known prior to delivery)?

3. Were you diagnosed prior to your child's diagnosis? If so, what were your feelings regarding your child while pregnant? After delivery, but awaiting diagnosis?

4. What was it like to hear that your child was also HIV+?

5. How has your child's illness affected you?

6. How has your illness affected your ability to take care of your child?

7. When you think of your child's future, what are you most worried about?

8. What are your hopes for you and your child?

9. Do you have other children who do not have HIV+? If so, can you describe your relationship with them?

10. Do you think that you will outlive your child?

11. If you die before your child, what kind of arrangements have been made for her/his care?

12. Do you feel that you have support? If so, can you describe the support?

13. What do you want others to know about mothers and children with HIV+?

ANALYSIS OF DATA

Matrix bins were the primary organizing structure of the interviews. The themes that are represented by the bins are: emotional reactivity at time of diagnosis; psychological integration of the illness; disease sequelae of HIV+/AIDS, that are currently present; development of a "will to live", or meaning in life; maternal attachment with children with AIDS, or who are potentially seropositive; and the relationship with children who are seronegative.

Sorting Data

The frame for interview analysis is modeled after the method used by Frey (1994) with some variation. The steps of data analysis included the following:

a. Transcription of the audiotaped interviews verbatim

b. Transcript coding

c. Construction of interview summaries

d. Assortment into matrix cells that elucidate mother/child attachment when the child has AIDS and when the child is AIDS-free and relationship to disease symptomatology and intrapsychic integration

e. Presentation of data

IV

Results

MAJOR RESEARCH FINDINGS

The research results will be reviewed in the following chapter, and they are organized within two sections that delineate the major themes that emerged from the study. The first section elucidates the ways in which the participants reacted intrapsychically to their diagnosis of HIV+/AIDS and have subsequently coped with this catastrophic illness, which in our society is associated with stigma. The second section describes the womens' relationships with their children who are seropositive, potentially seropositive and/or healthy. The study findings indicate that the psychological reactions of the participants corresponded to their disease trajectory. Heightened emotions were more likely to be associated with recent diagnosis and/or with AIDS-related illnesses and/or symptoms. Emotions abated during periods of reduced symptomatology. Psychological sequelae were also impacted by the presence or absence of emotional support, fear of disclosure, the development of a will to live, and the serostatus of the participants' children. Women whose seropositive status was known prenatally, were frequently encouraged to abort their unborn children. The majority of the participants considered abortion to be "murder." The women perceived their attachment to their children with AIDS to be intensified. They said that they cared for their seropositive children at the expense of their own health and conversely, looked to their seronegative children for emotional support and assistance with household tasks.

WOMEN AND HIV+/AIDS

Participants

Ethnic and psychosocial data. Thirteen women participated in this study. The women ranged in age from 24 to 40-years old, with the average age being 32-years old. Eight of the women identified themselves as Puerto Rican in culture and heritage. The five other women identified themselves as Irish, Norwegian, Indian-Irish or as culturally mixed. Eight of the women lived with men who they described as being their "husbands" or "boyfriends." The husband of one woman was in prison and she lived alone with their children. Five of the women revealed that their male partners had HIV+ or AIDS. Two men were seronegative and the serostatus of two others was unknown (one of whom had not been told of his partner's positive diagnosis). Two of the participants were widowed as a result of AIDS-related illness. The husband of one of the women had committed suicide. Ten of the participants lived in neighborhoods where poverty and violence prevailed. Several of the women had been recently burglarized.

All the participants were mothers, each having from one to six children. At the time of the interviews, four children had AIDS, two of whom grappled with severe AIDS-related medical problems. Three other children (ages 5 and under) had died as a result of AIDS. Two of these children were siblings. As is reported in Table II, the HIV+ status of other children was uncertain at the time of the interviews. Uncertain diagnosis was common in infants who were frequently tested for serostatus until they were one-year-old. Eight of the women reported that they were immersed in child care. One of these women had in-home support services for her child with AIDS. The children of three of the participants did not live with their mothers full-time and were cared for by extended family members.

AIDS-related status and history. Five of the participants tested positive for HIV+, the majority of whom (4) were asymptomatic. However, one of these women reported that she had experienced an AIDS-related illness and hospitalization and another reported that she experienced AIDS-related exhaustion. The dates of diagnosis and

HIV+/AIDS status of the participants are delineated in Table I. Three of the women learned of their seropositivity during pregnancy; one woman was diagnosed when both she and her infant were tested following childbirth. Two of the women learned of their positive diagnosis after their children (son, 15-months-old; daughter, 4-years-old) became extremely ill and were subsequently diagnosed with AIDS. Two women were tested positive after experiencing HIV+ related physical illnesses and/or symptoms. The remaining women learned of their seropositivity either after volunteering to be tested for money (1), following their partners' diagnosis (3), or as a result of intravenous drug use (1). The majority of the participants reported that they believed that they had become infected through sexual contact. One woman thought that she might have become infected through a blood transfusion, although the blood bank denied that possibility. The three other participants in the study reported intravenous drug-related infection.

AIDS-related symptoms. The most predominantly reported AIDS-related symptom was exhaustion and was reported to be a significant factor for eight of the women. Other physical symptoms that were reported were: diarrhea (2), weakness (3), cervical cancer (2), thrush (3), dizziness (1), weight loss (5), night sweats (1), lymphoma (1), leukoplakia (2), swollen glands (2), AIDS-related pneumonia (1), skin growths and irritations (1), spleen removal (1), herpes lesions (1), sinus problems (1), and tingling in toes (1). Four of the women suffered with severe and disabling AIDS-related medical problems, which prevented them from effectuating all but the simplest of daily living tasks.

AIDS-related losses. As indicated in Table I, most of the women in the study sample had experienced AIDS-related losses. The majority (11) had experienced the death of immediate family members, relatives or friends. Two of the women experienced the deaths of (3) children as a result of AIDS and (4) other women experienced the AIDS-related deaths of husbands or partners.

Table I: Demographics

	Age	Ethnicity	HIV+ Status	When Diagnosed	Partner HIV+	Supports	AIDS-Related Deaths
(1)	28	Puerto Rican	HIV+	1990	No	God	None
(2)	24	Puerto Rican	HIV+	1993	Unknown	God, Sister	None
(3)	29	Puerto Rican	AIDS	1989	No	Husband, Mother	Husband
(4)	40	Puerto Rican	AIDS	1987	Unknown	Daughter	Friends
(5)	36	Puerto Rican	AIDS	1994	None	God, Son, Mother	Boyfriend
(6)	28	Puerto Rican	HIV+	1990	None	God, Family	Friends
(7)	30	Puerto Rican	HIV+	1994	HIV+	Mother, Son	Friends
(8)	33	Indian-Irish	HIV+	1994	HIV+	Doctor	Cousin
(9)	37	Mixed	AIDS	1989	No	Family, Friends	Son, Friends
(10)	30	Norwegian	AIDS	1990	AIDS	Husband, Friends	Friends
(11)	34	Puerto Rican	AIDS	1988	HIV+	Sons, Partner	2 Children
(12)	40	Irish	HIV+	1992	HIV+	Children	Husband
(13)	27	Mixed	AIDS	1987	None	Mother	Husband

Current employment or work history. Two of the participants were employed at the time of the interviews. Another woman was enrolled in a college degree program in social work and was also employed part-time. One participant had been employed as a respiratory therapist until she became disabled by AIDS-related exhaustion several months before the study.

PSYCHOLOGICAL SEQUELAE
AND DISEASE TRAJECTORY

Initial Reactions to Diagnosis of HIV+/AIDS

Shock and denial. Initial reactions of shock, panic, rage and suicidality were described as being experienced from the time of diagnosis up to one year afterwards. The participants perceived the experience of having been diagnosed with HIV+/AIDS as being highly traumatic. The exact date of diagnosis was indelibly marked and remembered by even the women who had lived with AIDS for 8 years. Despite prior risk behavior, or knowledge of partner's seropositivity, 12 of the 13 women reported that they experienced extreme shock when told of their positive diagnosis. Many said that they felt "out of control." Reacting in disbelief, several women requested that the test be repeated. Their denial was frequently supported by physicians who also repeated seropositive tests in hope of laboratory error.

. One woman, whose serostatus was determined concurrently with that of her newborn, said, "I was floored . . . I had been so excited to have a little boy, a new baby . . . and then to find this out, I was shocked." Other women described their initial reactions to their diagnosis as:

You can't explain the words . . . you feel like you are falling . . . for the moment you feel everything is dark, like you are all alone.

You know, . . . it took a second to realize, because I looked to the midwife, "I have HIV?". . . Because she said, "You have this, and this, and this." But she didn't say, "HIV.". . . She just said the right name . . . And I looked to my social worker . . . and looked again to the other person, looked again at my midwife, and I said, "I have HIV?! No it's impossible!" I couldn't believe it.

When they first told me that I had the virus, I didn't understand what they were trying to say . . . When I first heard the bad news, I thought my baby was going to die, that I was going to die . . . I was very upset.

It was through my son's diagnosis that we found out about me . . . I had absolutely no idea that I was infected or that I was at risk . . .

To find out that this could happen to me, I was shocked!

Well, at first, I couldn't sleep . . . Thinking and thinking and thinking. I was so upset . . . I had to see a psychiatrist for pills.

Well, I knew the chance was there . . . I lived with a man that had it for 6 years and we never protected ourselves because I figured . . . that it couldn't happen to me. . . . I figured that after that length of time that I was safe.

I had no idea . . . I never would have thought that this would happen to me . . . After I got the positive diagnosis, I had two other tests done because I couldn't believe that it could be true.

Women who were intravenous drug users said that they reacted to their positive diagnosis in the following ways:

When they told me my results, I just flipped . . . I didn't think I was HIV+ . . . I just ran out and got high.

I was very upset . . . I cried and cried . . . I just didn't want to believe it.

A woman whose "boyfriend" was an intravenous drug user remembered,

> I wanted to die . . . It was hard for me because I had to sign for my baby . . . I thought I was going to lose my baby; everything I made in this world was gone in one second.

"I felt completely out of control because I was not expecting the diagnosis," remembered a woman whose "boyfriend" had died as a result of AIDS-related illnesses. Another woman remembered that after her "boyfriend" was diagnosed,

> I thought during the 2 week period . . . "I know I'm going to be positive . . . I've been living with him for a year, having sex . . . ," then the thought would go through my head that, "Well Magic Johnson's wife isn't positive . . . There might be a chance that I won't be." . . . I was already crying and hysterical and hyperventilating and ready to faint in the waiting room . . . I continued to cry harder and had to be helped out of there.

Only one of the participants reported momentary anticipation of a seropositive diagnosis. After 9 years of bi-yearly diagnostic assessments, she interpreted a difference in her physician's demeanor as confirmation of positive test results. Although she did not report experiencing shock at her own diagnosis, she remembered experiencing shock when her husband was diagnosed. "Well, I was shocked and hurt when he first got sick . . . Because we always kidded about it and said it could never happen to us."

Depression and anger. Four of the women reported feeling suicidal following their positive diagnosis. "I wanted to die . . . It was hard for me because my baby was 4 months old . . . " Only the sound of her infant's cry prevented her from taking the lethal dose of pills that she had in her hand. Another woman, who was diagnosed seropositive after her daughter's diagnosis said, "I was angry . . . I almost tried to kill myself because they told me by myself in the room. They just came out like that straight!" One individual, who had been diagnosed less than a year prior to the interview, stated that she was so depressed that she was barely able to get out of bed each day. Psychopharmacological treatment ultimately enabled her to cope with her diagnosis and illness. However, as she approached the anniversary of her diagnosis, she

Table II: Psychological Sequelae and Serostatus of Child

	Transmission	Why Tested	Reaction to Diagnosis	Psychological Sequelae	Child With AIDS
(1)	Sexual	Pregnancy	"Out of Control"	Anxiety, Anger	Two
(2)	Sexual	Infections	Shock	Denial	Uncertain
(3)	Sexual	Pregnancy	Shock	Acceptance	No
(4)	IV Drugs	Weight Loss	"Out of Control"	Acceptance	One
(5)	Sexual	Pregnancy	Shock, Suicidal	Anger, Depression	Uncertain
(6)	Sexual	Volunteered	Suicidal	Anxiety, Fear	Uncertain
(7)	Sexual	Pregnancy	Suicidal	Fear, Resignation	Uncertain
(8)	Sexual	Husband HIV+	Shock	Anger, Denial	No
(9)	Sexual	Son's Diagnosis	"Devastated"	Acceptance	One
(10)	IV Drugs	Volunteered	"Got High"	Anger, Depression	One
(11)	Sexual	Dtr's Diagnosis	Suicidal	Anger, Depression	Two
(12)	Sexual	Husband HIV+	"Out of Control"	Anger, Depression	No
(13)	IV Drugs	Volunteered	"Got High"	Anger, Depression, Fear	No

reported an upsurge of symptoms. Another woman, who was diagnosed seropositive during pregnancy remembered,

> They say, "You're pregnant," and you start laughing . . . Then they say to you, "But you're going to die . . . I don't know when." I thought the doctor was going to say that I was having twins! One thing is for the future and you're so happy about it, and the other thing is the end of your life and the world.

Being told her diagnosis in the gynecologist's office caused another woman to simultaneously confront life and death.

> I remember thinking . . . "there's all these pregnant women . . . all waiting to have good news about their babies and I'm coming out with a death sentence . . . I felt like my life was over and their's was just beginning.

PSYCHOLOGICAL SEQUELAE AND DISEASE TRAJECTORY

Time since diagnosis and AIDS-related illnesses. The psychological sequelae described by the study participants corresponded to the severity of AIDS-related symptoms experienced, and often to the length of time from diagnosis. Those who were more recently diagnosed (within 1 year), described experiencing more intrusive imagery and death anxiety than those who remained basically asymptomatic over 2-4 years. Women who were more recently diagnosed (whether or not disease sequelae were experienced) frequently feared impending death, and expressed feelings of fear and alarm.

Death Anxiety. Although all the women expressed death awareness, many perceived their diagnosis as an immediate death sentence. Death anxiety was heightened when they were symptomatic.

> You don't know when you are going to die . . . I'm so scared. I don't know if I'm going to wake up or if I'll be dead in that bed.

> Well, when you first get the results, you want to die. So I just lay there, because I was going to die.

> I was waking up in the night and going over in my head how I was going to die and my funeral and this and that . . . I wasn't getting any sleep. . . . My initial thought was that I had a few months. I didn't care whether they told me 5, 7, 10 years, I thought, "I'm dying. This is it."

> I'm just waiting for death. Just waiting, it's going to happen. It has been 8 years, and I feel that I'm starting to get sick now. I have been having a lot of weight loss, and I have been very sick.

Death anxiety and AIDS-related losses. Death anxiety and depression were exacerbated in women who had experienced AIDS-related deaths of family and/or friends and who had witnessed the wasting syndrome characteristic of AIDS.

> I remember the last time I walked into her room and she was very sick . . . she was laying on her side and her Johnny had fallen open, and she had a diaper on and the space between her legs was like a huge . . . space. I mean, there was no meat! I just looked and I couldn't believe it! . . . I thought, "Oh my God, if my kids ever see me laying there like that! I just couldn't take it."

Depression and despair. Feelings of depression, anger and despair corresponded to the level of AIDS-related symptomatology present and, frequently, to the degree of emotional support and understanding received or anticipated. Feelings of hopelessness, fear and foreboding were frequently experienced.

> I don't feel good a lot. . . . Sometimes, I just don't even care. I mean I wouldn't take my life or anything but I just wish that it would end. I am sick of living like this. . . . I just wish that the time would come so I wouldn't have to worry. I would be ready to go.

One woman described her depression and dearth of hope, "I get depressed because I'm having a bad day and don't feel good and I start thinking, "Is this the way it is going to be? It's a beautiful day out and I can't go out because I don't feel well." Anticipated fear of rejection and subsequent isolation contributed to the depression experienced and described by the following women:

> I worry sometimes that when I get sicker, their father won't bring them to see me like that, and I always have this fear that they're going to back away from me just like I did to the other lady . . . because they won't be able to cope with seeing me sick, and that bothers me. It's a fear of dying alone.

> Mothers may have AIDS, but they still love their children just the same. They should not be shunned. What they need is just the opposite. They need to be supported, not pushed away.

A 27-year-old woman with AIDS described her fervent need to process her feelings with her mother, whose own denial prevented her from responding empathically to her daughter's plight and thus, contributed to her anger and despair.

> Knowing that you have a terminal illness . . . My Mom says, "You might live for 15 years." I tell her, "Get serious, it has been 8 years, there are not many who live over 10!" Even my doctor told me that. Most die within 10 years. It is true and she won't believe it. I mean, look at me! Can you see me? I mean, I tell her, "What the hell!" She is in denial. I can't talk to her. "I can get hit by a car tomorrow," she says. But that it's totally different. I would rather get hit by a car than wake up each day knowing that I have a terminal illness and that I am dying.

Fear of disclosure. Fear of disclosure prevented some of the women from obtaining the psychosocial support and assistance with household tasks, that they so intensely needed. For them, the price of disclosure exceeded the benefit of potential support and was reality based, for many. One woman described the reactions of her husband's family after she and her children were diagnosed with AIDS. "My husband's family has totally rejected them since they found this out . . . They don't kiss them anymore, they don't go to see them at the hospital, . . . they don't do things together like they used to." Fear of discovery of their seropositive status extended, in one case, to a woman's husband. "I thought 20,000 times about telling him, but I can't figure out how. If the baby is positive, then I will have to speak with him and just somehow get the courage and strength." As their illnesses progressed and the women became more symptomatic, fear of disclosure escalated.

> I don't want anyone to know. Sometimes people slip. I didn't even tell my Dad . . . I was scared that he would be scared to hug me or give me a glass of orange juice.

> It would be horrible if there were specific hospitals for people with AIDS, like in some countries, and people were labeled as AIDS patients . . . I have never said I have AIDS.

> There are a lot of people who don't know about AIDS. They worry that by touching something I touched they could get it. They say things like, "That person has AIDS. I better not sit there!"

> I would scream to the four corners of the earth, "Yes, I am HIV+." But I'm protecting my kids. When the people say, "You have HIV+," I say, "Me? You crazy!"

> I know if my boss ever found out, my job would be over. People don't know; they don't understand.

Several women said that, for them, fear of disclosure was linked with the way they had been treated by some professionals in the medical community.

> It's bad when people know that you have HIV+. . . . When my little boy was sick, I took him to the hospital. The doctor didn't close the door and was standing right there and say, "You know that your son

has AIDS?". . . And when I went to the hospital to get checked, the doctor screamed that "I don't work on people who have the virus!"

I went to the dentist one time. He take out my teeth, and I told them the truth, that I was HIV, you know? And they treat me real bad. They took out my tooth, yeah, but they make me clean my blood in the cup with water.

Acceptance. Heightened emotions abated in women who had been asymptomatic for a long period of time, as they were able to intrapsychically integrate living with a life-threatening illness. Those who experienced few AIDS-related symptoms or illnesses, or whose symptoms interfered minimally with daily functioning, reported fewer feelings of anxiety, anger and depression than those who felt debilitated by the disease. There were able to focus on "fighting" AIDS, or to find other meaning in life. Once again, the presence or absence of psychosocial support also impacted the degree of adjustment.

It was so hard in the beginning. But now, I feel better. One day at a time.

Sometimes, I feel like getting down, you know, that I'm not going to live . . . but then I say, "No, you can't be that way!" And I get up and fight!

I don't fear being HIV+ because you don't necessarily have to have AIDS to die. You can get pneumonia and die. HIV+ is there . . . but I don't fear for me because I'm pretty healthy and I hardly ever get sick.

Psychological sequelae and maternal attachment. Definitive relationships could not be established between the womens' psychological reactions to their own disease process and the way in which they bonded with their children. Although the study findings did indicate psychological sequelae that corresponded to the disease trajectory, a clear representation of the impact of these emotions on attachment was not described by the participants. Furthermore, the women who were most disease symptomatic were not the sole care givers for their children. As a result, the relationships of these women and their children could not be attributed only to the interplay between the disease process and psychological sequelae.

Resilience

Working through/ the will to live. Those who were able to see and/or make meaning out of their situation, to develop a will to live, were able to go on with their lives as People With AIDS. They did not focus on death nor did they deny its possibility. They overcame the initial oscillation between intrusive emotions and denial, and subsequent periods of anger and depression, by developing their own "will to live." "I'm definitely not ready to die. No way! I'm not afraid of dying. It's not something that I'm frightened of. But I can't, because I have things to do. I refuse!" Several of the women spoke publicly about AIDS education and prevention. "I spoke at junior high schools until my lips were ready to fall off and my throat hurt."

The women who participated in AIDS support groups and organizations felt that these activities both gave meaning to their lives and provided them with support. Several women developed meaning from their participation in the study in hopes that other women would benefit from their forthrightness. "I was happy to do it because I feel like there's other people who have the same thoughts, and fears and hopes that I have."

I hope that other mothers get to hear what I have to say . . . because really my life is a tragedy and so is my daughter's. People need to really think before they act . . . and drugs and alcohol is a very, very big part of people getting infected today. Because when you start drinking, you don't think about using protection.

I want to tell those girls who are the same like me to hang in there. Have a lot of faith and take care of the kids, and pray to God that there is a cure . . . You have to fight! If you don't fight, and you just throw yourself in bed, don't eat . . . you are going to disappear. I have the faith that there's going to be a cure.

One woman developed meaning in her seropositive status by committing to overcome her drug addiction as a consequence of her diagnosis.

> I think HIV saved my life. Because if not, I'd still be out on the street shooting drugs, you know? And getting into more trouble than I was already into. You know, who knows what was next for me? . . . Now my life is stabilized. I'm happily married. I have very good physicians for me and my daughter.

All the women whose children were either seropositive, potentially seropositive, or whose children had died as a result of AIDS, expressed an unwavering commitment to their children that became their will to live.

> I dedicated my life to my kid. I said, " I don't care about me, I want my baby to live . . . I used to give him meals at the proper time, play with him, give him love, be there for him, every time he used to cry, I used to be holding him. I mean, I dedicated every single thing I could do for him . . .

> She's my baby. She's my life. She's the one that keeps me going. I don't keep me going. She does . . . she's the boss. I was going to do the best thing I can do for this baby so it didn't come out with this sickness.

> I put the kids first. I had to be there for them.

> My children are my life.

> When I feel depressed, I take my kids in my arms and I hug them.

> I was a good mother to my kids. I was there for them until they died. I never let anyone take my kids away from me . . . I brought them into this world and I was there for them until they died.

I feel kind of good about Johnny's life . . . He had a very happy life. When he was alive, we tried to give him as many experiences and things that we could. If there was something he wanted to do, or something he maybe wanted to do when he grew up, we made sure he got a chance to do it.

Creating a beautiful grave site became the meaning for a woman who anticipated the imminent death of her 3-year old daughter.

I'm right now working on getting money together for Diana's grave site. I already have it picked out. And I went and saw it and looked around and liked it. And it's very beautiful, right by a frog pond. And it's very sunny, so I liked it.

Spirituality. Many of the women developed spiritual meaning in their dilemmas. They (9) believed that their faith supported and empowered them as they navigated their disease trajectory and that of their children.

Putting faith in Jehovah is what helped me. Because I know when Jehovah put a hand in the situation, it helps you pull things together . . . God is not going to give you something more than you can handle it.

I have not been emotionally effected because I have faith and I go to church regularly.

I've been a Christian now for over 2 1/2 years and that's really made a big difference in my life.

Ultimately, it's God's will, whatever God wants . . . but I do ask God for things and for help.

Familial support. The existence of supportive families who were willing to listen to the fears and concerns of the women contributed to resilience.

I have a lot of support from my family. My Mother just left to go to Puerto Rico recently, after coming here to help me. My grandparents, they are always calling me. My uncle . . . a lot of my family is backing me up.

My family is supportive. They're not really that close by, but also my husband's family is very supportive . . . even though we're separated. I have . . . a wide network of friends and acquaintances around the HIV and AIDS thing. And that offers a lot of support . . . A couple of years ago . . . one of the local newspapers did a story, a very positive story . . . and plastered it on the front page. Most people . . . know I'm HIV+ . . . I can't imagine trying to live with this as a secret. I know people who do that and I think that it would be so incredibly hard.

Summary of Psychological Reactions. Despite prior risk behavior, the majority of women reported that they experienced shock and disbelief when diagnosed with HIV+/AIDS. In the period following their diagnosis they commonly experienced anger and depression; several were suicidal. Regardless of projected life expectancy, the diagnosis of HIV+/AIDS was perceived as an immediate death sentence and precipitated a period of intense death anxiety. Death anxiety was exacerbated in those women who had experienced AIDS-related losses and had witnessed the deterioration that they perceived as prophesying their own. Psychological symptoms escalated as the disease trajectory progressed or when emotional support was not forthcoming. Women expressed the need for emotional support and the need to talk about their AIDS-related fears and feelings. Fear of disclosure frequently obstructed means of having these needs met. Heightened emotions abated in the women who experienced fewer AIDS-related illnesses and who developed the will to live or meaning in their predicament. The will to live was often linked to religious belief and dedication to their children. Supportive families, who were willing to speak openly about HIV+/AIDS, helped facilitate psychological adjustment.

VERTICALLY TRANSMITTED HIV+/AIDS

Pregnancy and Attachment

Prenatal concerns. Eight of the women were confronted with the potential seropositivity of unborn children. Five of the women were pregnant when they were diagnosed with HIV+/AIDS and three subsequently became pregnant following confirmed seropositive status. None of the women chose abortion, although they reported having been pressured by medical personnel to terminate their pregnancies. They perceived their unborn children to be living beings. Many of the women reported that they concentrated on special prenatal regimes in order to provide their children with healthy starts. These regimes frequently included herbal medicines, which were perceived to be disease fighters.

Most (7) of the women who were prenatally aware of their seropositivity felt that God's will determined the serostatus of their child. Those who were diagnosed during pregnancy, and who anticipated healthy babies, described greater prenatal anxiety than those who were aware of their serostatus prior to conception. The women who were aware of the potential for vertical transmission, prior to conception, defended against the possibility that their child would be diagnosed with AIDS. They focused on the "low" rates of vertical transmission and on prenatal treatment with AZT. The desire for children coupled with the belief that the percentages favored a seronegative outcome, enabled most of the women to maintain hope that their child would be healthy. "I was thinking that he was going to be alright." One of the women remembered that she had been "scared but tried not to think about it." Another woman remembered,

> They told me the percentage of her becoming positive and I just thought God would stand by my side. I took AZT and the doctors said it was only a 15% chance of her being positive. They believe she would have remained negative if I didn't have placenta previa. It was the hemorrhaging that infected her . . . I didn't think much about it. I was thinking about the joy of having a daughter.

Anticipated loss. Although all of the women spoke of their concern for their unborn infants and of the healthy standards they attempted to maintain, several women anticipated a poor pregnancy outcome and anticipated that their children would have AIDS. Another woman experienced a mixture of hope and foreboding and said that she constantly worried about her unborn child throughout the pregnancy.

> I cried and worried about whether I had done the right thing . . . having the baby and having to die . . . he would be sick and then die. It was going to be terrible for me . . . But then in another way, I say, "What about if he comes out negative and then I kill him?"

> I was more worried about him through my 9 months of pregnancy. I knew what I had; I knew the chances that I had, that my baby had.

Abortion. All of the women who were pregnant while aware of their seropositive status, viewed abortion as tantamount to "killing." Although abortion was recommended to them, their strong views against it, their desire for children, combined with faith, and the belief that the odds favored a healthy pregnancy outcome, eliminated the possibility. In addition to their philosophical views on abortion, women who were seropositive during pregnancy, also reported feelings of attachment to their unborn children. Attachment was reported to be fostered by prenatal knowledge of their infant's gender. The participants described their feelings about abortion and attachment in the following statements:

> It's already there, and I felt the baby move. How I going to kill something, somebody, that little person who's moving?

> I didn't care about me, but the baby, I didn't want to kill the baby.

> Under no circumstances would I have considered abortion because I was very hopeful that this time it would be a boy. One eye, two eyes, one ear, two ears, didn't matter.

> It was my baby and I was going to keep it.

It wasn't a planned pregnancy, but I've never considered an abortion, although I'm concerned about the baby's health. I don't think it's appropriate to kill the baby because it's God's will.

Abortion just wasn't an option.

When they told me I was HIV+, they offered me an abortion, . . . I don't believe in abortion . . . everybody has a right and this baby has a right to be born. He was going to be born. I said, "No matter how he comes out, he's going to do it." I tried to do the best thing I could do for this baby so he didn't come out with this sickness.

I don't believe in abortion. I've always wanted a baby.

If I knew that I was HIV+, I would never have a child. I would try not to even get pregnant because I don't think it's right to bring somebody to suffer or to walk the same steps that we got to walk suffering . . . But if you're pregnant, that's different.

Concerns for other children while pregnant. The women whose seropositive status was prenatally diagnosed worried more about their older childrens' serostatus than that of their unborn children. They either felt that they could protect their unborn children with their own interventions or that a seropositive diagnosis was inevitable.

I was going to do the best thing I can do for this baby so it didn't come out with this sickness, but in the moment, I was more worried about my daughter. I started to realize that I had the signs in her pregnancy, the swollen glands, the fever . . .

You see the baby, you think, "He's going to die. What am I going to do?" Then I say, "No, he's going to be fine." It was worse for the 2-year-old because I already had him and loved him so much . . . and he's adorable.

Another woman reported that she "hoped against hope" that her 6-year-old daughter would not have AIDS, while simultaneously "preparing" herself for the positive diagnosis of her unborn child.

> I was told that it was more likely that the baby would be positive so I was prepared. They told me it would take 3-6 months before they'd be able to tell me, but the baby was sick right away, and by the time she was 1 1/2 months old, I knew she was HIV+.

REACTIONS TO THE DIAGNOSIS AND DISEASE PROCESS OF PEDIATRIC AIDS

Five of the women interviewed had children with pediatric AIDS or had experienced the death of children as a result of AIDS (three children of two mothers died). The participants described the following psychological reactions to their childrens' disease process.

Shock and denial. Four of the women said that they experienced shock, disbelief and horror when their children were diagnosed with pediatric AIDS. They reported that learning of their child's diagnosis was far more crushing to them than learning of their own serostatus.

> I was devastated. I was in shock. It was a real surprise. You know, it wasn't anything that I had expected.

> It was worse when I heard my son was positive than when I learned that I myself was positive. The doctor had to give me a sedative of some kind.

> I felt very bad. I cried. I was very afraid. I had hoped against hope that they would be negative.

> When they told me that he was positive, I didn't understand what they were trying to say. I thought he just had a virus . . . then they explained to me that he had the antibodies. I thought that my baby was going to die. I was very upset.

Daily survival was the primary concern of another woman, after her daughter was diagnosed with AIDS because at the time of her child's birth, she did not have any clothing, furniture or shelter. The need to provide rudimentary essentials for her sick child motivated her to take control of her life.

> I definitely didn't take it as with a grain of salt. But I wasn't in shock either. I said to myself, "Okay, now I really have to stand up and fight! And now I'm not fighting just for me, I'm fighting for her too."

Anger and depression. Watching their children suffer with the disease elicited feelings of anger and depression. "Well, everyday, I would think, 'He can't possibly be any worse. He can't possibly survive another 24 hours,' and he would. And that was really hard." "Every time I see my kids suffering, it get me mad . . . " "I can't imagine how it is going to feel to watch him get sick and decline." "I know Diana doesn't have much of a future. I just think about what virus is going to hit her . . . And I just hope it doesn't take her eyesight from her, or brain damage." Seeing her son contend with the disease and its implications, caused ubiquitous pain for another woman who said, "Seeing him there daily, dealing with medications . . . there's a saying in Spanish that says, "If the eyes don't see, the heart doesn't feel."

Several mothers endured the agonizing period of waiting for their child's serostatus to be determined, which required a series of blood tests. The uncertainty of their child's diagnosis resulted in anticipated loss and depression. "I was very happy to have my little boy and really sad at the same time because I knew what was coming."

> They send me because it was one from the baby, they say was positive. So after the positive is coming three negatives. My daughter, they told me she was negative, that everything came out good, and I started crying . . . I was crying, and crying, and crying. Those people don't know that every time I go there to have something, my heart is on the floor broken.

> Well, I was worried. Like in the first test they do, it takes about a month for you to know the results. So that month, you like, thinking,

"What's going to happen, yes, no?" You see the baby, then you think about, "Well, he's going to be sick, he's going to die."

Guilt and bargaining. Guilt was expressed by some, but not all of the study participants. Method of transmission did not correspond with the presence or absence of guilt. One of the women, with a history of drug use, stated that , "I went through a big thing of guilt for over a year, and I was back and forth into the hospital, the psychiatric unit, dealing with the guilt that I had made my daughter infected." Women who contracted HIV+ from sexual contact also expressed feelings of guilt.

> I feel really guilty about having brought the children into the world now that I know I have AIDS and the children are going to die because of it.

> You want to give them more love . . . But sometimes I hit them. I don't want to because I'm not going to be with them when they grow up.

After she learned that she had AIDS, another woman looked at her 2-year-old daughter and told her that she was "sorry." "I wanted the best thing for my kids, and I can't do it." In penance, another woman bargained with "God" for seronegative status for her son in exchange for growing her hair for one year. However, guilt was not a factor for another woman,

> . . . you hear sometimes people talking about . . . maybe the guilt mothers might have for having transmitted this disease to their children. And that was never really an issue for me . . . People think that mothers are guilty, feel guilty. I don't believe they are.

Sick Mothers Caring for Sick Children

Stress and exhaustion. The intensified stress that commonly accompanies caring for a chronically and terminally ill child, was exacerbated by the mothers' own illness-related limitations and emotions. The women described experiencing overwhelming exhaustion, that was as much a function of their own disease process as it was related to the care taking demands of their child with AIDS. The mother of two children who died of AIDS recounted, "It was real hard because I never slept. I was always taking care of them, trying to feed them, change the breathing machine . . . " A mother whose son was diagnosed with AIDS at 15-months- old and who died when he was 5-years-old, remembered the struggle of caring for him as she grappled with her own AIDS-related illnesses.

> . . . taking care of him was a huge job. He had to have his medications, his tube feedings, frequently he wouldn't be well so I would just sit and hold him in the afternoon . . . I had to carry him all the time . . . He matured intellectually and emotionally but not physically . . . The amount of energy and time and intensity involved in taking care of him was like having a baby for 5 years . . . When I had my spleen out . . . I had a lot of fatigue . . . I remember lying on the couch in the afternoon and falling asleep and not being able to stay awake to watch the children, who were two and four. And that was a terrible, frightening feeling, knowing that you couldn't stay awake to watch them.

Another mother described the way in which she contended with AIDS-related exhaustion and caring for her children.

> You give the bottle to the baby, boom to the bed again. It's hard for me. You have to rest. Because I feel like everything is falling over me . . . even breathing is hard for me. . . . I'm so tired . . . I fight with my little one to go to sleep. I fight with my daughter, who gives me a hard time, to take a nap. Let the other ones do what they want outside . . . so I can rest . . .

Hopelessness and resignation characterized the feelings of one woman whose children have AIDS. "What can we hope? Their future is in God's hands." A woman who was recently diagnosed with AIDS during pregnancy described her feelings.

My kids suffer because I'm angry. I want so many things and everything is coming backwards . . . It's one emotion on top of the other one . . . I don't know why I'm angry. The only thing is, I wanted the best for my kids and I can't do it. I'm pretty angry and my kids are the ones suffering because I scream at them. I lost my patience a long time ago.

Mother/Child Attachment and Pediatric AIDS

Anticipated grief and intensified attachment. Anticipated loss was reported by mothers whose children were seropositive or potentially seropositive. "I knew they were going to die . . . The other kids, I didn't worry about them because they're okay and they are going to school. The babies never had a chance to go to school." Hypervigilance in regard to immunity and disease exposure, and worry about impending death concerned all the mothers whose children had AIDS, had received a false-positive diagnosis (2), or whose diagnosis was uncertain (3). "You know, she's got it so bad that . . . it seems like anything could kill her." In anticipation of their childrens' death they hoped for developmental milestones, and periods of normalcy for their children. These hopes were both simple and yet colossal. One mother hoped that her 3-year-old daughter would survive until her fifth birthday. She also hoped that she would be able to walk unassisted before she died.

I really don't have any big expectations for us because I would be expecting something that would never come true, and I don't want to set myself up for failure.

All the mothers whose children were diagnosed with AIDS desired to do special things with their children before their anticipated death.

I've given my daughter the best life I could give her. I went out and we did Make-A-Wish. And I bought her toys, and I don't know if you've seen her room yet . . . She has a beautiful canopy bed and we're going to, me and my husband, are going to paint the ceiling

with angels. We're going to paint angels so they glow in the dark,
and stars and a moon.

He wanted to be a farmer or a heavy equipment operator. And so he
did. He would always go to the farm . . . so he had plenty of chances
to be in the barn with the cows. His uncle would worry about him
being in the barns because of his immune status, but it was more
important for him to have that.

The women commonly anticipated that their sick children would
die before them. They felt that the threat of loss intensified their
relationship, and the bond between them. The mothers whose children
had AIDS, or had died as a result of AIDS, all described intensified
attachment towards these children. Several women said that they
experienced "remarkable bonds" with the child whose illness they
shared. "She's, you know, somehow more in my heart . . . " "You want
to give him more love, you want to be more there for him." "They need
you more now than ever. . . ."

The women said that they focused on the needs of their children
with AIDS rather than on their own, even when faced with the extreme
exhaustion that is characteristic of AIDS. They reported that they
frequently checked on their children during the night and prepared
special foods for them.

Knowing that she is dying, that she may not be with us tomorrow, we
do everything with her, although she's very limited. She can't go to
the pool, she can't get a lot of sun, she can't be in the heat . . . she's
got it so bad, it seems like anything could kill her. She needs more
support and affection.

When he was very little, I was very attentive. Every time he was in
bed, I'd go check him and keep him awake to make sure everything
was okay. I was very worried about him as a baby.

I took care of my two kids. I didn't leave them in the hospital for
other people to take them to a foster mother. I was there for them
until they were 5 . . . My girl got sick . . . and I left my house and

went to another state because there was a good doctor there. And I
went all the way there to see if they can give my girl more time,
because back home they told me she had only 6 months to live. So I
told my husband and we packed our stuff and we went to the other
state, and they gave my girl 3 more months to live.

It's made us closer. There definitely was one point where I tried to
get away from her and make a distance, and I had to realize she was
my responsibility, and she was my daughter. And I was hurting her
and I was hurting me at the same time . . . we have a remarkable bond
between us today.

I pay more attention to him . . .

I do worry more about him than the other children.

Degree of disease symptomatology seemed to intensify the
attachment between the women and their children. One woman reported
having a closer bond with her daughter who had end-stage AIDS, than
with her son who had HIV+ and was asymptomatic. "She is somehow
more in my heart and we live what moments we have with her to the
fullest." Another woman whose 5-year-old daughter died in 1991 and
whose 5-year-old son died in 1991 (both due to AIDS) requested that
her remains be cremated and spread over the graves of her two children.
Their common illness was a connector. A similar attachment was
described by a woman, whose son died as a result of AIDS when he
was 5-years-old.

Johnny and I were very, very close. Probably more so, because he
was sick . . . there was a special closeness with me and John . . .
Johnny knew that he and I shared this, that we had the same
disease . . . I always had really strong feelings about being there for
him . . . I couldn't save his life, but I could be there when he needed
me.

Concern that others would not take care of her son, in the way that she
did, prompted this woman to hope that he would die before she did. The

belief that their children needed them was echoed by most of the women, who worried about the potential for their children to be AIDS orphans.

> I wanted to outlive him. I didn't want . . . obviously I did not want him to die, but I didn't want to die and leave this child who needed me, who is sick, without a mommy.

Children as providers of support. The women expected that seronegative children (8-years-old and older) would help them with household tasks and with the physical demands placed upon them by their younger children. They were also expected to help care for their younger siblings with AIDS. One woman, whose younger children both had AIDS, said, "When my son was 13, he helped me with the little girl and with my baby—the boy. He was a good helper." Other women did not receive the same assistance from their children.

> My older kid, he's 13. I thought when I told him what's going on, he could have been helping me take care of the house, helping me with all the kids, if he was positive thinking. He's not helping me . . . He wants to hear nothing about HIV+ when I try to talk to him.

Children were also expected to provide empathy and emotional support. None of the women reported that their children were willing or able to fulfill this need. Several women expressed anger and frustration about their childrens' unwillingness to speak with them about AIDS, and their feelings about their physical deterioration.

> I was kind of shocked that my children don't treat me like I'm fragile . . . I thought they'd coddle me more . . . worry every time I coughed and everything. They ignore me. They just act like there's nothing wrong with me.

The following is the way a 9-year-old boy reacted to his mother's disclosure that she had AIDS,

After I told him, he was very cold and bitter towards me. He had no feeling . . . And I hope he has a different way of treating me because he really hurt me a great deal . . . he didn't come over to me, to hold me or anything. . . . My husband was yelling at him, saying, "Can't you see what you're doing to your mother?"

Another woman described her attempt to speak with her 8-year-old son about her seropositivity,

He only wants to play . . . but I try to talk to him . . . to teach him to be, if I'm not here, to learn to do things so he could do it by himself . . . to be a real man. He helps me a lot with the other kids. Sometimes I talk about my feelings with him.

One mother hoped that her children would listen as she described her AIDS-related limitations to them,

. . . they don't really talk about it. They won't discuss it. They just try to act like it doesn't exist.And I'll say stuff . . . because they're always trying to push me to do more and more and I can't . . . and they always gripe at me.

Several of the mothers understood that their childrens' inability to provide emotional support to them was symptomatic of their own grief process.

I think he angry with me maybe cause I'm going to leave him, you know? Even I say I going to try all the best I can do to care of myself to last . . . at least one more year or 2 more years . . .

Another woman empathized with the fear and pain that her 6-year-old son felt when she tried to talk with him about her illness. "About 3-months ago, I tried talking to him about it but he was suffering too much, saying, 'Oh Mom, please, please don't die! Please don't die.'" She said that she attempted to soothe her son, and decided to delay the conversation until some time in the future.

In five of the families, older children were intended to be the primary care givers of younger siblings, when their mother died. One woman hoped that she would live until her twin daughters were 18-years-old so that they could be responsible for their younger sister. "Every year gets closer to when they are going to be 18 . . . and they can take care of their sister, or even if they're 16 or 17." Another woman had arranged for her older daughter to care for her 9-year-old son with AIDS.

> I have a 20-year-old daughter who knows what's going on and will be the one who would take care of everyone if I get sick. I'm more worried that they will take my son away from my daughter.

Summary of Maternal Attachment and Vertically Transmitted Aids

The study participants reported that, when prenatally aware of their own seropositive status, they took better care of themselves in order to minimize the chances of vertical transmission. Through their religious convictions many of the women embraced the belief that, ultimately, "God's will" would determine the serostatus of their child. Although abortion was recommended to them, 12 of the 13 women interviewed believed that abortion was equivalent to the murder of their children.

The women said that they experienced far greater distress when their children were diagnosed with AIDS, than when they themselves were diagnosed with HIV+/AIDS. They felt that the anticipated loss of their children, coupled with the fact that they shared the same illness, intensified the bond between them. Some, but not all, of the women experienced guilt about vertical transmission.

All the women reported that they focused on the needs of their children with AIDS, before their own. However, many of the women also experienced the extreme physical exhaustion, that is characteristic of AIDS. Their own disease process frequently prevented them from providing optimum care to their children. Physical limitations, coupled with the care taking needs of sick children, resulted in their dependence on seronegative children (some as young as 8-years-old) for task assistance as well as emotional support. Although several of the women understood that their children's own psychological processes impeded their ability to provide emotional support to their mothers, the majority of the women experienced anger and frustration, when their children were unwilling or unable to meet their expectations.

SUMMARY OF RESEARCH FINDINGS

Despite knowledge of risk, the majority of the women interviewed reported that they experienced shock and disbelief when diagnosed with HIV+/AIDS. The diagnosis was perceived as an imminent death sentence, by most of the women.

Psychological sequelae were associated with the disease trajectory and the length of time from diagnosis. Psychological adjustment to this chronic, terminal disease was facilitated by familial support, spirituality, and a "will to live, " which was frequently developed through caring for their children with AIDS. Although medical professionals encouraged the pregnant women with AIDS in this study to consider abortion, the women felt that they would be killing their children, should they consent to the procedure. Intensified attachment was described between mothers and their children with AIDS. Although they perceived to put the needs of their sick children before their own, the disease sequelae frequently prevented them from caring for their children optimally. Fear of disclosure, societal stigma, and isolation not only exacerbated psychological sequelae, but also prevented the women from obtaining the assistance that they needed. Therefore, they frequently sought out their seronegative children for help with care giving and household tasks, and for emotional support. For the most part, these children were unable to provide their mothers with the assistance that was needed.

V
Discussion

Women, most of whom are economically disadvantaged, are the fastest growing group of People With AIDS in the United States. The majority of women with HIV+/AIDS are Africa-American or Latina and live in urban areas, where they experience the constant threat of violence. Survival issues are compounded by AIDS-related fear of disclosure, and social and familial stigmatization and disenfranchisement. This study showed that women with HIV+/AIDS endure physical and psychological sequelae concomitant with this catastrophic illness, while they also care for their sick and dying children, without receiving the emotional and physical support that would reduce their suffering.

Cultural values and expectations regarding children, combined with psychological denial concerning the outcome of high risk behavior and/or powerless in heterosexual relationships, has resulted in the increase of children with AIDS. The rise of pediatric AIDS in this country is in proportion to the increase in numbers of women with AIDS. The disease process in children with AIDS is generally quicker and more virulent than in adults, in which differences have also been found between men and women. The literature on potentially terminal childhood illness (Bowlby, 1973, 1980; Futterman & Hoffman, 1973; Natterson, 1973; Rando, 1986) reports that parental attachment with ill children is usually intensified until the parent accepts that the situation is terminal, at which time decathexis occurs. Parkes (1988, 1983) disputed the contention that anticipated loss resulted in decathexis and instead, claimed that intensified attachment is a consequence of death that is foreseen. The results of this study corroborate the findings of Parkes. The women who were interviewed reported hypervigilance regarding their children's symptomatology and health, and the existence of an intensified bond as a result of their common illness, or the potential of this illness.

The diagnosis of HIV+ in themselves and in their children was reported to be highly traumatic and the beginning of a mourning process, of which the study participants were in various phases/stages. Preliminary findings indicate a correlation between the disease and mourning process, and a connection between these processes and interpersonal relationships. Interpersonal relationships were frequently characterized with increased emotional neediness and anger. The findings of Andrews (1993) indicate that mothers with AIDS depended on their children, who were seronegative, for emotional and care giving support. The finds of this study confirmed those results. Corroborating the research of Sarwer and Crawford (1994), the women in this study reported intensified relationships with their children with AIDS, and that they cared for them at their own physical expense. Thus, as hypothesized, anticipatory grief functioned to intensify the mother/child relationship regardless of the physical and psychological stage/phase of illness. Many of the women developed a "will to live (Frankl, 1984) by caring for their sick children. Others ultimately integrated the illness in their lives and developed a sense of themselves as AIDS educators, thus deciding not to be subordinated to the disease or to their suffering as is described as resilience by Higgins (1994).

The major findings of this qualitative study elucidate the ways in which women with AIDS psychologically responded to their own disease process, to their children with AIDS, and to their children who are seronegative. The diagnosis of HIV+/AIDS was perceived as being traumatic and unexpected (regardless of past or current risk behavior). The emotional reactions to the disease trajectory mirrored the grief process. Psychological sequelae were related to the presence or absence of AIDS-related symptoms and illnesses, the availability of emotional support, and the development of a "will to live."

Women reported intensified bonds with their children with AIDS (especially when the children were symptomatic). The women said that they neglected their own health in order to care for their seropositive children, and that this care giving frequently gave their life meaning, and facilitated their "will to live." The women reported to be most debilitated by AIDS-associated exhaustion, which often impeded their ability to care for their children, regardless of serostatus. Caring for their children with AIDS, whose physical development was frequently impaired, and who were were immunologically vulnerable and sick themselves, was extremely difficult. Mothers looked to healthy children for emotional support and assistance with household tasks, and experienced anger and frustration when the children were unable to provide this help.

Twelve of the thirteen women who were interviewed stated that they felt that abortion was an unacceptable procedure for them, and that they likened it to murder. This position was reinforced by their religious convictions that maintained that every child had a "right" to be born, and that the serostatus of their child would be determined by "God's will." In addition to their spiritual convictions, the women, who were prenatally aware of their seropositive status, believed that the maintenance of healthy regimes during pregnancy would help to prevent vertical transmission of AIDS.

The findings indicate a correlation between the disease trajectory and the mourning process, and a preliminary association between psychological sequelae and attachment. These psychological processes seem to be influenced by the child's seropositivity and anticipated grief. Further research is needed to definitely confirm this connection.

Emotional Sequelae of HIV+/AIDS

As was reported by the women interviewed, depression and suicidal ideation are common problems for people with AIDS (Zegans, Gerhard & Coates, 1994). Other emotions that were expressed by the participants and found in the research (Zegans et al.; Septimus, 1990), include distractibility and agitation, emotional lability, angry outbursts, withdrawal and apathy. Although these feelings are commonly associated with the mourning process, traumatic experiences, and catastrophic illness, AIDS dementia could also account for these emotions (Worden, 1991; Zegans et al.). Septimus also reported feelings of helpless and subsequent depression in women with AIDS, that were also reported by the study participants.

While many of the participants expressed feeling angry, only several of the women expressed feelings of guilt (or self recrimination). Lifton (1980) concludes that anger becomes a way of experiencing life force by attacking others instead of the self. Rando (1993) states that ". . . it appears the survivor is more comfortable dealing with anger than with guilt or any other form of severe anxiety (p. 585)." Anger and frustration about children who were not emotionally empathic, or lack of understanding by other family members were common themes. Guilt about leaving children as AIDS orphans was expressed less frequently.

Diagnosis of HIV+ perceived as traumatic. As Doka (1993) and Horowitz (1986) assert, all the study participants perceived the diagnosis of HIV+ as being traumatic. Doka claims that an individual diagnosed with a life-threatening illness will respond as she/he would to any major trauma. Figley (1995) defines trauma as an immediate threat. Regardless of the method of transmission, the women who were interviewed described their reactions to the diagnosis of HIV+ as being immediately threatening and terrifying. Many of them described feeling suicidal, alone and vulnerable, and feeling as though they had been given an immediate death sentence. McCann and Pearlman (1990) conclude that the diagnosis of a life-threatening illness disrupts the individual's schemas related to invulnerability, and that the diagnosis of AIDS is particularly traumatic in this regard. Doka (1993) and Horowitz (1986) state that people who have been diagnosed with life-threatening illnesses are generally less emotionally responsive and less interested in interpersonal relationships. Many of the women reported isolating behaviors out of fear of disclosure and stigmatization. They were very desirous of speaking about their feelings regarding AIDS and their own disease process, but reported finding little verbalized interest from family or friends. When conversations were initiated, the women felt that they experienced minimal empathic support.

Herman (1992) and van der Kolk (1987) assert that when the trauma is severe, no person is immune to the effects. They conclude that the traumatic experience results in an interpersonal vacillation between withdrawal and dependence. Corroborating the claims of van der Kolk and Herman, the women in this study reported greater egocentricity and increased neediness for emotional support and assistance with physical tasks, simultaneously with detachment from those who were perceived as judgmental and not helpful. Although some of the women who knew of their seropositivity reported initial detachment during pregnancy, all the women subsequently reported intensified attachment with, and focus on, their seropositive children.

Grief and mourning. The traumatic outcry that the diagnosis of HIV+ or AIDS precipitated, triggered the mourning process in the women interviewed. They reported experiencing mourning over their current losses, the ultimate loss of life, and the anticipated loss of their children. The work of Sarwer and Crawford (1994) also conclude that people with AIDS respond to their disease in coping stages that mirror the grief process. Grief functions to untie the psychological bonds that connect the bereaved person to the loved person, or to their own life (Lindemann, 1979; Raphael, 1983; Rando, 1986). Rando (1993) asserts that the psychological process of mourning is similar across class and ethnic groups, as was found in this study. No differences in grief or trauma responses were reported by the women in the study, regardless of their ethnic differences. The grief process has been delineated in phases (Rando, 1996), tasks (Doka, 1990) and stages (Kubler-Ross, 1969; Sarwer & Crawford, 1994). The use of these delineations is a contextual framework from which to conceptualize the psychological reactions of women with AIDS. The categories are not fixed or linear, and there is frequently movement back and forth between stages/phases as was found in this study.

The findings of this study corroborate the general findings of Kubler Ross (1969), Doka (1993) and Rando (1986) that predict a correlation between the trajectory of a chronic life threatening illness and intrapsychic integration that parallels the grief process. The study results corroborate those of Sarwer and Crawford (1994) which connect the psychological sequelae associated with HIV+/AIDS with Kubler-Ross's stage model of coping with a terminal illness. The women who were interviewed reported emotional reactions that coincided with the stages (Kubler-Ross, 1969, Sarwer & Crawford, 1994), phases (Rando, 1986, 1993), or tasks (Doka, 1990) of the mourning process. Integrating these conceptualizations with trauma theory (van der Kolk, 1987; Horowitz, 1986; Doka, 1993; Herman 1992) and the study findings, the following delineations were found. The time of diagnosis or avoidance phase (Rando, 1993) was experienced with shock, avoidance, egocentricity and anger frequently directed at family members. More anger was expressed by the study participants who were either newly diagnosed or most AIDS-related symptomatic. The living-dying interval, or the confrontation phase (Rando, 1986), was experienced by heightened emotions and vacillation between death acceptance and death denial. Bargaining for health and longevity for self and/or child in exchange for personal sacrifice was common during this period, especially during periods of remission. Two women were able to establish new identities and accept the disease process as is described in connection with the accommodation phase (Rando, 1996; Crawford, 1994; Kubler-Ross, 1969).

Rando (1986) attested that long-term anticipation of loss coupled with increased need for care ultimately resulted in physical exhaustion and emotional detachment from the dying person. She proposed that relief was a common reaction after the death of a loved one suffering from long-term chronic debilitating illness. The theoretical position of Parkes & Weiss (1983) that anticipatory grief serves to intensify attachment was confirmed, refuting Rando's (1986) conclusion that anticipatory grief that lasts longer than 18 months frequently results in decathexis or emotional detachment from the dying person. The women whose children either had died as a result of AIDS-related illness, had AIDS, or whose diagnosis was uncertain all reported experiencing intensified attachment and hypervigilance with these children. Perhaps, the fact that parental loss of a child has been reported to be the most severe death from which to recover (Rando, 1986; Raphael, 1983) also served to intensify maternal attachment, when that loss was anticipated. The anticipated loss coupled with the common bond that mothers with AIDS verbalized experiencing with their seropositive children might explain the study findings, which refute the literature on parental reactions to pediatric chronic terminal illness (Futterman & Hoffman, 1973; Natterson, 1973; Bowlby, 1973, 1980; Rando, 1986).

Increased attachment and pediatric AIDS. Lifton (1980) reports that the self is severed from psychic compassion for others when confronted with death. Bowlby (1973, 1980) proposed that the greater the threat of loss of the interpersonal bond, the greater the attempt to maintain the attachment. The research on parental reaction to life-threatening illness in their child (when the disease is not vertically transmitted) reports internal turmoil that is marked by oscillation between clinging and distancing (Futterman & Hoffman, 1973; Natterson, 1973; Bowlby, 1973, 1980; Wertz, Fanos & Wertz, 1994). Wertz, et al. also found that parents generally became overprotective with their sick children. Serban (1989) reported overprotection of children who are sick, or at risk for illness, and that this behavior is a compensatory attempt to ward off the guilt that is experienced as a result of genetically transmitted disease. Although overprotective behavior was reported by the women interviewed, the presence of guilt can only be hypothesized as it was not overwhelmingly reported. The study results confirmed the findings of those researchers who specifically investigated reactions of mothers who have vertically transmitted AIDS (Armistead & Forehand, 1995; Melvyn & Sherr, 1993; Geballe, Gruendel & Andiman, 1995). Their findings, and the findings of this study, indicate that seropositive women experience an intensified attachment with their seropositive children and that they indeed experience empathy and compassion for them, as they neglect their own needs to care for their children. Armistead and Forehand, Melvyn and Sherr, and Geballe, Gruendel and Andiman also found that mothers focused on the health needs of their children, while neglecting their own health. Study findings indicated that the women experienced difficulty caring for their sick child while they also coped with their own disease sequelae, as was reported by Geballe et. al. As was also reported by Andrews, Wiliams, and Neil (1993), the women interviewed stated that while focusing on their children's needs was taxing for them, it also gave them a reason to live and increased their self-esteem.

As was reported by Andrews et al.(1993), many of the Latina women interviewed had not disclosed their seropositivity to their children, nor did many of the children know their own diagnosis. Mothers expressed concern that the children would not be able to handle the gravity of the diagnosis, and also reported that they were fearful of disclosure, should their children reveal their seropositivity to others.

Women With AIDS, and Pregnancy

Abortion was considered tantamount to murder and was not considered a viable option by any of the study participants, who were prenatally aware of their seropositivity. Armistead and Forehand (1995) also reported findings of conflictual beliefs surrounding abortion, and predicted that women would continue pregnancies after diagnosis of seropositivity. Other studies on pediatric AIDS report that women knowingly became pregnant, when aware of their seropositivity, because they perceived the risk of vertical transmission to be low (Ybarra, 1991; Stuber, 1992; Levine & Dubler, 1990; Armistead & Forehand, 1995). The cultural expectation for Latina women to bear children (Julia, 1989; Ramos-McKay, 1988), coupled with the meaning that was developed in caring for their child (that was not culture specific), and the stated feeling that the child had "a right to be born", influenced most of the women in this study to either become pregnant or remain pregnant after positive diagnosis of HIV+/AIDS.

Relationships with Children Who Were Seronegative

Corroborating the findings of the Andrews (1993) study, women reported depending on children who were as young as 8 years old for emotional support and household tasks. Seronegative children also assisted the women in care taking their children with AIDS. Mothers reported feelings of anger and detachment when their healthy children were unable to be supportive of them, or when the children expressed their own feelings of anger and/or fear about their mothers' seropositivity. However, the women reported that the children were more likely to express their negative feelings behaviorally than verbally, and that this was difficult for the mothers to bear. Nevertheless, when asked about future plans for surviving children, some of the women reported that their older children would be responsible for care taking their younger siblings.

Differences Between Transmission Methods and Emotional Reactivity

The number of women who were intravenous drug users in this study sample was not large enough to draw any major conclusions from the research. However, those interviewed did report exacerbated drug use at the time of diagnosis of HIV+, as has also been reported in the literature (James, 1988; Meintz, 1989). James also reported that diagnosis and adaptation to HIV+ was impaired by coexisting substance abuse disorders, and that women who were intravenous drug users bonded poorly with their children. The small number of women who were IV drug users did confirm initial difficulty focusing on their infant if the mothers were actively using substances at the time of birth. However, several of the women also stated that they used their relationship with their children to turn their drug use around, as was reported by Armistead and Forehand (1995).

Research Experience

Finding participants and collecting data were both difficult, and at times, frightening in this study. The program directors who were initially contacted were either concerned that their clients had been inundated with research requests (although the studies were usually pharmacologically focused), or were unwilling to do more than post an announcement of the study in their agency. After contacting the directors of the programs with whom the study participants were associated, it became necessary to gain approval and methodology suggestions from other staff before the research could proceed. As a result, attempts to locate potential study participants took almost 6 months before initial contact was made. Although all the participants reported that they benefited from their participation, accessing them was made difficult by the understandable intent to protect people with AIDS and by the initial hesitancy of potential participants. Even when programs supported the research, only a small number of women contacted, ultimately agreed to participate.

Although making contact with prospective participants was difficult, one of the women who participated in the study argued that her participation was essential to the research, and for herself. She learned of the study through a support group associated with the Visiting Nurses Association. Although HIV+ was transmitted to her when her children were too old to have been possibly effected, she stated that her seropositivity did in fact impact her relationship with them, and that it was very important to her that she be permitted to participate. Although she did not meet the study criteria of having children who either were seropositive or who were potentially seropositive, she was included in the study due to her persistence that her voice needed to be heard as a mother with AIDS.

The daily problems faced by women with AIDS, given the demographics and disenfranchisement of the population, coupled with their medical needs and those of their children, resulted in many missed or rescheduled interview appointments. At least 25 attempts were made to complete 19 interviews. While interviewing some of the women in their homes enabled them to participate in the study, it also exposed this researcher to the daily violence and risk that many of the women face. At any one time, the environmental background included gang members, pimps, and/or drug dealers. Entering some of the graffiti decorated buildings, required walking past gangs and entering through hallways that were littered with glass from broken windows and doors. Several of the women stated that they had either been recently robbed or that they feared a break-in. It would be amiss to report these findings without indicating that this researcher was fearful of robbery or attack during portions of the research process. When in the homes of the participants, this researcher experienced anxiety and concern about safely leaving the premises and finding her automobile intact.

Safety considerations resulted in this researcher's attempt to dress in a nonobtrusive manner in order to attract minimal attention, and to be more aware of environmental cues. As part of the study, the women revealed their innermost concerns and feelings to this researcher. In doing so, a relationship was fostered that resulted in secondary-traumatization, as this researcher worried about their futures and felt helpless about their current plights. The faces of the courageous women, who faced daily battled yet were willing to participate in this study so that other women might be better understood, are indelibly marked in this researcher's mind.

Limitations of Study

The small sample size, that resulted from the difficulty experienced in obtaining study participants, and the fact that the sample was not randomly selected, limits the generalization of the research findings. Further, while statistics do show an increase in disease transmission through heterosexual contact, the majority of women with AIDS, in this country, become infected through intravenous drug use. As the majority of sample participants contracted HIV+ through heterosexual contact, the findings of the study may not be entirely representative of women with AIDS in the United States. Nevertheless, it is also this researcher's opinion that, while method of transmission can be useful information, the way in which the participants and their children are currently affected by AIDS is far more significant.

The validity of the study results is also limited by use of the phenomenological approach, whereby the perceptions and accounts of the participants are described as accurate findings. In fact, the study results indicate the women's constructions of the way in which they have reacted to their own disease process, and the way in which their relationships with their seropositive and seronegative children have been subsequently affected. They believed that they experienced greater attachment towards their seropositive children and, despite grappling with debilitating disease sequelae, attempted to put the needs of their sick children above their own. Although this researcher could not ensure that their accounts were completely objective, it was apparent that the women felt committed to their children.

> Whatever the socioeconomic level, ethnic group, or type of family structure, we have yet to meet a parent who is not deeply committed to ensuring the well-being of her or his child. Most families are doing the best they can under difficult circumstances; . . . (Bronfenbrenner, 1979, p. 849).

Although the women in this study might not have been able to provide optimum care for their healthy or seropositive children, they intended to do so, and struggled with feelings of guilt or despair when they could not.

The study results may be somewhat skewed due to the fact that all the participants were connected with health care programs specifically related to AIDS, that several of the study participants were AIDS activists, and that caseworkers persuaded some of the women to participate. For example, both of the women who responded to a letter sent out by a New England pediatric HIV+ program located in a medical center, were outspoken advocates of AIDS education, and had publicly disclosed their HIV+ status. The fact that most of the women to whom the letter was sent did not respond may indicate that the responses were not representative. Conversely, the Latina women, who were approached by their caseworkers, may have agreed to participate due to the personal nature of the request. While not apparent in the research findings, the presence of the interpreter in the room, when interviewing the Spanish speaking women, may have influenced the responses given because of fear of disclosure.

More in-depth findings might have been gleaned if the participants all agreed to second interviews and if multiple measures had been used, such as depression, self-esteem, or parenting inventories. As the past trauma history of the participants was not elicited, it is unclear whether pre-morbid experiences exacerbated emotional responses to disease process, or to attachment.

The characteristics of the study sample, in terms of the stages of disease trajectory, was not evenly distributed or clear enough to comment definitively about the impact of the mourning process on maternal attachment, when vertical transmission occurs. The debilitating nature of AIDS, combined with the numerous care taking requirements during the final stages, would most likely limit the number of women willing to participate in such a study.

Lastly, the fact that the majority of women with HIV+ or AIDS are Latina or African American (Andrews, William, & Neil, 1993; Antoni et al., 1992; Dane & Levine, 1994; Krieger & Margo, 1994; Levine & Dubler, 1990; Stuber, 1992; Ybarra, 1991) highlights the importance of investigating the impact of HIV+ and/or AIDS on this population. However, while the theoretical literature on complicated and anticipatory mourning alludes to the concept of multiculturalism, the accepted theorists on complicated and anticipatory grief (Bowlby, 1980; Horowitz, 19486; Lindemann, 1979; Parkes & Weiss, 19483;

Rando, 1986. 1993; Raphael, 1983; Worden, 1982) present a view that is more fundamental, and ignores cultural implications. Therefore, a limitation of the study is the way in which the accepted theories influence the analysis of the research.

IMPLICATIONS FOR FURTHER PSYCHOLOGICAL RESEARCH

The results of this proposal suggest several areas for future psychological study. In that the majority of participants reported awareness of risk behavior prior to their own seropositive diagnosis, research is needed to determine effective methods of disseminating AIDS education and prevention, as well as effective means of persuading people to use this information. This research should take place in local communities, with the assistance of residents, in order to be most efficacious. This research could be viewed as a pilot study, that would provide methods of influencing other vulnerable populations, such as adolescents, to eliminate behaviors that expose them to HIV+/AIDS transmission. In addition to determining ways in which to educate people about AIDS prevention, this researcher feels that it is imperative to study ways in which to better assist people who are already struggling with this illness.

Studies that elucidate cultural and religious values and attitudes with regard to mothering and abortion, and HIV+/AIDS, in the Latina and African-American communities are recommended. The dissemination of this information could provide medical professionals and AIDS educators with the necessary knowledge to treat their clients with sensitivity and understanding. A longitudinal study of the relationship between the HIV+/AIDS disease process, intrapsychic integration, and attachment would be beneficial. The usefulness of this data for the medical field, which works with women and children with HIV+ and AIDS is compelling. Studies that are more directly connected with pediatric HIV+ programs, or are based out of hospitals might provide easier accessibility for participants and result in larger study samples. Research into the emotional and physical needs of women with AIDS is essential in order to ascertain the ways in which mothers could be supported, without relying on their healthy children. It would be incumbent on the researchers to determine the types of emotional support that were needed and that women would accept.

The research findings indicated that psychological adjustment was related to the development of meaning and the"will to live." Research on resiliency and meaning-making in this population is recommended in order to learn ways that other women might be assisted in navigating through their disease process with greater psychological ease.

Research into the maternal responses to infants with Fetal Alcohol Syndrome and Neonatal Abstinence Syndrome would enable psychologists and other health care providers to assist these mothers in caring for their infants, and might be useful for those who work with women with AIDS whose children are seropositive.

Further research is also recommended to ascertain the psychological sequelae and needs of seropositive children and those who have been orphaned by AIDS.

RECOMMENDATIONS

This research highlighted the need for societal commitment to improve the quality of the lives of women and children with AIDS, and children who are potential AIDS orphans. As long as most of the women and children, who are must vulnerable to disease transmission, live in poverty, they will continue to face daily survival issues that, for them, transcend the risk of AIDS and simultaneously increase their vulnerability. Culturally sensitive support needs to be available to women who are fearful of confronting male partners about safe sex and/or who are fearful of revealing their seropositive status to them.

More extensive and locally based educational programs are needed that focus on AIDS prevention, education, and the disease process itself. Given the current understanding of the way in which stress can accelerate the disease process, it is imperative that ways of reducing stress in women with AIDS are determined and implemented. Accurate information regarding methods of transmission and the disease trajectory are essential so that People With AIDS can live with this chronic illness, without stigma, and with reduced stress. In order to be effective, educational programs will need to consider cultural values and differences in their design. It is recommended that they take place within communities and that they focus on information transmission through personal contact, rather than the dissemination of written material.

It is imperative that training for those who work with women and children with AIDS include information about cultural and community values and attitudes about abortion. An understanding that women with AIDS do indeed love their children, but are frequently impacted by their own physical and psychological AIDS-related sequelae, as they care for their children, is critical. Psychoeducation about the interplay between the physical trajectory of chronic terminal illness and psychological sequelae is essential in order to promote empathy for women with AIDS as they navigate in the world.

In that all of the women interviewed expressed the need for support, sensitive assistance with child care would probably be welcomed and valued. An in-home support program is recommended to provide assistance with household tasks, care giving to young children, and emotional support to the women involved. The focus of this program would be the needs that the women themselves delineated, and would not focus on health-related issues (such as obtaining blood samples, etc.) or health-related concerns of their seropositive children (as these services are already provided by agencies such as the Visiting Nurses Association). As a result of secondary traumatization that can occur when confronted with the pain and trauma of others, this program should include de-briefing and supportive components for the staff.

In conjunction with the development of support programs for women with AIDS, family therapy is recommended for families grappling with issues of need, catastrophic loss and disclosure. In-home psychotherapy would be most beneficial because many women reported that their increased AIDS-related symptomatology precluded the ability to participate in support groups, that were already available in the community. As part of in-home psychotherapy, families need assistance in processing and making arrangements for the future care of children who would potentially be AIDS orphans. Lastly, as all of the women reported the time of diagnosis to be traumatic, and as they reported being told of their child's seropositivity without the presence of psychological support, it is recommended that programs be developed and implemented that provide this service to women with AIDS. The service should include follow-up contact within the week after diagnosis, and at regular intervals thereafter. As would be recommended for any professionals working with people who are coping with catastrophic illness, staff support and de-briefing would be essential components of this program.

Appendix
Consent Form

Project Title: Vertically Transmitted HIV+/AIDS: The Impact on Maternal Attachment

Interviewer: Sharon Walker, Psy.D.
Telephone# (603) 357-3848, Ext. 19

1. The purpose of this research is to ascertain the ways in which potentially vertically transmitted HIV+/AIDS (when the mother has been diagnosed as positive) effect the mother/child relationship.

2. The results of the research could improve the services available to mothers and children with HIV+/AIDS.

3. If you are 16 or older and agree to participate in this study, I will ask you questions about your illness and your child's illness (if your child has been diagnosed with HIV+ or you are awaiting diagnosis) that could potentially upset you.

4. If you agree to participate in this study and Spanish is your preferred language, a translator will participate in the interview and will hear your answers. The interpreter will be bound by confidentiality.

5. If you agree to participate in this study, you will be asked to complete a one hour interview with me today and a 15 minute debriefing interview one week from today. Both interviews will be audiotaped.

6. If you agree to participate in this study, you will be paid $25.00 at the initial interview.

7. If you participate in the study and complete the two interviews, I will contact you by telephone approximately 10 days after the final interview to answer any questions that you might have.

8. If you are upset by your participation in the study, I will provide you with a list of referrals to counselors or psychologists who are familiar with issues associated with HIV+/AIDS. I will obtain this list from the agency or program with which you are already affiliated.

9. The results of the study will be published in a bound dissertation. Anonymous quotations from the interviews will be included in the final project and could be included in subsequent published articles.

10. All responses will be kept strictly confidential. No information will be released that would expose the identity of any participant. In order to preserve confidentiality:

—all audiotapes and transcriptions will identify you only by a code number, not name.

—the tapes will be transcribed by a paid typist; they will be identified only by code.

—you will be offered the audiotapes after they have been transcribed; they will be destroyed if you do not want them.

—I will analyze the transcribed tapes (with code numbers only)

—Consent Forms and any other material with your name on it will be kept in a locked file at my office.

11. The research involves no more than minimal risk.

12. Participation in this study is voluntary and you may withdraw at anytime during the interview process.

13. If you have any questions about this research, you may contact me at (603) 357-3848, Ext. 19.

14. I willingly volunteer and consent to participate in this research project.

Signature of Client

Printed Name of Client

References

Andrews, S., Williams, A. B., & Neil, K. (1993). The mother-child relationship in the HIV-1 positive family. *Image-Journal of Nursing Scholarship, 25*(3), 193-198.

Antoni, M. H., Schneiderman, N., LaPerrier, A. O'Sullivan, M. J., Marks, J., Efantis, J., Skyler, J., & Fletcher, M. A. (1992). Mothers with AIDS. In P. I. Ahmed (Ed.), *Living and dying with AIDS* (47-85). New York: Plenum Press.

Arimistad, L. & Forehand, R. (1995). For whom the bell tolls: Parenting decisions and challenges faced by mothers who are HIV seropositive. *American Psychological Association, 2*(3), 239-250.

Berg, B. L. (1989). *Qualitative research methods.* Needham Heights, Massachusetts: Allyn & Bacon.

Birn, A. E., Santelli, J., & Burwell, L. W. G. (1994). Pediatric AIDS in the United States: Epidemiological reality versus government policy. In N. Krieger & G. Margo (Eds.), *AIDS: The politics of survival* (89-107). New York: Baywood.

Bowlby, J. (1973). *Attachment and loss.* New York: Basic Books.

Bowlby, J. (1980). *Loss: Sadness and depression.* New York: Basic Books.

Bowlby, J. (1982). *Attachment.* New York: Basic Books.

Bronfenbrenner, U. (1979). Contexts of child rearing: Problems and prospects. *American Psychologist, 34,* 844-850.

Brown, G. W. & Harris, T. (1978). *Social origins of depression.* London: Tavistock.

Canosa, C. A. (1991). HIV infection in children. *AIDS Care, 3*(3), 303-309.

Carovano, K. (1994). More than mothers and whores: Redefining the AIDS prevention needs of women. In N. Krieger & G. Margo (Eds.), *AIDS: The politics of survival* (pp. 111-125). New York: Baywood.

Cates, J. A., Graham, L. L., Boeglin, D., & Tielker, S. (1990). The effect of AIDS on the family system. *Families in Society: The Journal of Contemporary Human Services, 71*(4), 195-201.

Centers for Disease Control. (1995, April 7). *AIDS Weekly Surveillance Report,* AIDS Program, Atlanta, Georgia.

Centers for Disease Control (1996), *AIDS Weekly Surveillance Report,* 8(2), AIDS Program, Atlanta, Georgia.

Chesney, M. A., & Folkman, S. (1994). Psychological impact of HIV disease and implications for intervention. *Psychiatric Clinics of North America, 17*(1), 163-179.

Cohen, F. L. (1993). The epidemiology of HIV infection and AIDS in women. In F. L. Cohen & J. D. Durham, (Eds.), *Women, children and HIV/AIDS.* New York: Springer.

Cohen, F. L. & Durham, J. D. (Eds.). (1993). *Women, children and HIV/AIDS.* New York: Springer.

Coleman, M. (1991). Pediatric AIDS: The professional responsibilities of child care givers to children and families. *Early Childhood Development and Care, 67,* 129-137.

Comas-Diaz, L. & Griffith, E. E. H. (Eds.) (1988). *Clinical guidelines in cross-cultural mental health.* New York: John Wiley & Sons.

Dane, B. O. & Levine, C. (Eds.). (1994). *AIDS and the new orphans.* Connecticut: Auburn House.

Danieli, Y. (1985). The treatment and prevention of long-term effects and intergenerational transmission of victimization: A lesson from Holocaust survivors and their children. In C. R. Figley (Ed.), *Trauma and its wake* (pp. 295-314). New York: Brunner/Mazel.

Davidson, L. M. & Baum, A. (1986). Chronic stress and posttraumatic stress disorders. *Journal of Consulting and Clinical Psychology (54),* 3, 303-308.

Doka, K. J. (Ed.). (1989). *Disenfranchised grief: Recognizing hidden sorrow.* Massachusetts: Lexington Books.

Doka, K. L. (1990). Grief education: Educating about death for life. In G. Anderson (Ed.), *Courage to care.*(285-293). Wash. D. C. : Child Welfare League of American, Inc.

Doka, K. J. (1993). *Living with life-threatening illness: A guide for patients, their families and caregivers.* Massachusetts: Lexington Books.

Doyal, L., Naidoo, J., & Wilton, T. (Eds.). (1994). *AIDS: Setting a feminist agenda.* Bristol, Pa.: Taylor & Francis.

Faltz, B. G. (1992). Coping with AIDS and substance abuse. In P. I. Ahmed (Ed.), *Living and dying with AIDS* (137-150). New York: Plenum Press.

Federal Regulations. Protection of human subjects. Title 45, Part, 46, National Institute of Health (1991).

Fee, E. & Krieger, N. (1994). Thinking and Rethinking AIDS: Implications for healthy policy. In N. Krieger & G. Margo (Eds.), *AIDS: The politics of survival* (pp. 227-277). New York: Baywood.

Figley, C. R. (Ed.). (1985). *Trauma and its wake volume 1.* New York: Brunner/Mazel, Inc.

Fox, N. A. (1988). The effects of prematurity and postnatal illness on the mother-infant interaction: A study of a high-risk dyad. In E. J. Anthony & C. Chiland. (Eds.), *The child in his family: Perilous development: child raising and identity formation under stress* (pp. 211-223). New York: John Wiley.

Frankl, V.E. (1984). *Mans' Search for Meaning.* New York: Washington Square Press.

Freyberg, J. T. (1980). Difficulties in separation-individuation as experienced by offspring of Nazi Holocaust survivors. *American Journal of Orthopsychiatry, 50*(1), 87-94.

Frey, L. (1994). *The psychological and sociopolitical sequelae of HIV infection in women.* Unpublished doctoral dissertation, Antioch New England Graduate School, Keene, New Hampshire.

Frierson, R. L., Lippman, S. B., & Johnson, J. (1987). AIDS: Psychological stresses on the family. *Psychosomatics, 28*(2), 65-68.

Futterman, E. H. & Hoffman, I. (1973). Crisis and adaptation in the families of fatally ill children. In E. J. Anthony & C. Koupernik (Eds.), *The child in his family* (pp. 127-145). New York: John Wiley.

Geballe, S., Gruendel, J., & Andiman, W. (Eds.), (1995). *Forgotten children of the AIDS epidemic.* New Haven: Yale University Press.

Garcia Coll, C. T. & de Lourdes Mattei, M. (Eds.) (1988). *The psychosocial development of Puerto Rican women.* New York: Praeger.

Giacquinta, B. S. (1989). Researching the effects of AIDS on families. *The American Journal of Hospice Care, 6,* 31-36.

Goodheart, C.D. & Lansing, M.H. (1997). *Treating people with chronic disease: A psychological guide.* Wash. D.C.: American Psychological Association.

Gorman, C. (1994, July 4). Moms, kids and AIDS: Can testing and treatment before and after birth help thousands of youngsters threatened by HIV? *Time*, 60-65.

Harrison, H. (1983). *The premature baby book.* New York: St. Martin's Press.

Herman, J. L. (1992). *Trauma and recovery.* New York: Basic Books.

Higgins, G. O. (1994). *Resilient Adults.* San Francisco, Ca: Jossey-Bass.

Horowitz, M. J. (1986). *Stress response syndromes.* Northvale, N.J. : Jason Aronson.

Irish, D. P. Lundquist, K. F., & Nelsen, V. J. (Eds). (1993). *Ethnic variations in dying, death and grief.* Wash. D. C.: Taylor & Francis.

James, B. (1994). *Handbook for treatment of attachment-trauma problems in children.* New York: Lexington Books.

James, M. (1988). HIV seropositivity diagnosed during pregnancy. *General Hospital Psychiatry, 10*(5), 309-316.

Janoff-Bulman, R. (1992). *Shattered assumptions.* New York: The Free Press.

Julia, M. T. M. (1989). Developmental issues during adulthood: Redefining notions of self, care, and responsibility among a group of professional Puerto Rican women. In C. T.Garcia Coll & M. de Lourdes Mattei (Eds.). *The psychosocial development of Puerto Rican women.* New York: Praeger.

Kalichman, S.C. (1995). *Understanding AIDS.* Wash. D.C.: American Psychological Association.

Kaltenbach, K. & Finnegan, L. P. (1988). The influence of the neonatal abstinence syndrome on mother-infant interaction. In E. J. Anthony & C. Chiland (Eds.), *The child in his family: Perilous development: Child raising and identity formation under stress* (pp. 223-231). New York: John Wiley.

Kaplan, D. N. , & Mason, E. A. (1960). Maternal reaction to premature birth viewed as an acute emotional disorder. *American Journal of Orthopsychiatry, 30*, 539-552.

Klaus , M. H., & Kennell, J. H. (1982). *Parent-infant bonding.* Missouri: C. V. Mosby.

Krieger, N. (1994). The histories of AIDS. In N. Krieger & G. Margo (Eds.), *AIDS: The politics of survival* (pp. 223-227). New York: Baywood.

Krieger, N. & Appleman, R. (1994). The politics of AIDS. In N. Krieger & G. Margo (Eds.), *AIDS: The politics of survival* (pp. 3-55). New York: Baywood.

Krieger, N. & Margo, G. (1994). Women and AIDS. In N. Krieger & G. Margo (Eds.), *AIDS: The politics of survival* (107-111). New York: Baywood.

Kubler-Ross, E. (1969). *On death and dying.* New York: Macmillan.

Kubler-Ross, E. (1987). *AIDS: The ultimate challenge.* New York: Macmillan.

Kurth, A. (1993). Reproductive issues, pregnancy, and childbearing in HIV-infected women. In F. L. Cohen & J. D. Durham (Eds.), *Women, children and HIV/AIDS.* (104-135). New York: Springer.

Levine, C. & Dubler, N. (1990). HIV and childbearing: Uncertain risks and bitter realities: The reproduction choices of HIV-infected women. *The Millbank Quarterly, 68*(3), 321-351.

Lifton, R. J. (1983). *The broken connection.* New York: Basic Books.

Lindemann, E. (1979). *Beyond grief: Studies in crisis intervention.* New Jersey: Jason Aronson.

Martin, J. L. (1988). Psychological consequences of AIDS-related bereavement among gay men. *Journal of Consulting and Clinical Psychology,56,* 856-862.

Mayers, A. & Spiegel, L. (1992). A parental support group in a pediatric AIDS clinic: Its usefulness and limitations. *Health and Social Work, 17*(3), 183-191.

Mays, V. M. & Cochran, S. D. (1988). Issues in the perception of AIDS risk and risk reduction activities by black and Hispanic/Latina women. *American Psychologist, 43,*(11), 949-957.

McCann, I. L. & Pearlman, L. A. (1990). *Psychological trauma and the adult survivor.* New York: Brunner/Mazel.

Meintz, S. (1989). The human right of bonding for warehoused "AIDS babies." *Family and Community Health, 12*(2), 60-64.

Melvin, D. & Sherr, L. (1993). The child in the family—responding to AIDS and HIV. *AIDS Care, 5*(1), 35-42.

Miller, D. (1994). *Women who hurt themselves: A book of hope and understanding.* New York: Basic Books.

Miles, M. B. & Huberman, A. M. (1984). *Qualitative data analysis: A sourcebook of new methods.* Newbury Park, California: Sage.

Natterson, J. M. (1973). The fear of death in fatally ill children and their parents. In E. J. Anthony & A. Koupernik (Eds.), *The child in his family: The impact of disease and death* (pp. 121-125). New York: John Wiley.

Nestler, V. M. & Steinhausen, H. C. (1988). The offspring of alcoholic mothers: Subsequent development and psychopathology of children suffering from fetal alcohol syndrome. In e. J. Anthony & a. Koupernik (Eds.), *The child in his family: The impact of disease and death* (pp. 231-243). New York: John Wiley.

O'Connell Higgins, G. (1994). *Resilient adults overcoming a cruel past*. San Francisco: Jossey-Bass.

Olson, R. A., Huszti, H. C., Mason, P. J., & Seibert, J. M. (1989). Pediatric AIDS/HIV infection: An emerging challenge to pediatric psychology. *Journal of Pediatric Psychology, 14*,(4), 1-21.

Panter-Brick, C. (1991). Parental responses to consanguinity and genetic disease in Saudi Arabia. *Social Science and Medicine, 33*(11), 11295-1302.

Parkes, C. M. (1988). Research: Bereavement. *Omega, 18*(4), 365-372.

Parkes, C. M. & Weiss, R. S. (1983). *Recovery from bereavement*. New York: Basic Books.

Patton, M. Q. (1980). *Qualitative evaluation methods*. California: Sage.

Ramos-McKay, J. M., Comas-Diaz, L. & Rivera, L. A. (1988). Puerto Ricans. In L. Comas-Diaz & E. E. H. Griffith (Eds.) *Clinical Guidelines in cross-cultural mental health*. (204-233). New York: John Wiley.

Rando, T. A. (1984). *Grief, dying and death: Clinical interventions for caregivers*. Illinois: Research Press.

Rando, T. A. (Ed.). (1986). *Parental loss of a child*. Champaign, Illinois: Research Press.

Rando, T. A. (Ed.). (1986). *Loss and anticipatory grief*. Massachusetts: Lexington Books.

Rando, T. A. (1993). *Treatment of complicated mourning*. Champaign, Illinois: Research Press.

Raphael, B. (1983). *The anatomy of bereavement*. New York: Basic Books.

Rim, Y. (1991). Coping styles of (first and second generation) Holocaust survivors. *Personality and Individual Differences, 12*,(12), 1315-1317.

Sanders, C. M. (1989). *Grief: The mourning after*. New York: John Wiley & Sons.

Sarwer, D. B. & Crawford, I. (1994). Therapeutic considerations for work with persons with HIV disease. *Psychotherapy, 31,* (2), 262-270.

Seibert, J. M. & Olson, R. A. (Eds.). (1989). *Children, adolescents, & AIDS.* Lincoln: University of Nebraska Press.

Seidman, I. E. (1991). *Interviewing as qualitative research.* New York: Teachers College Press.

Septimus, A. (1990). Caring for HIV-infected children and their families: Psychosocial ramifications. In G. Anderson (Ed.), *Courage to Care.* (91-106). Washington D.C.: Child Welfare League of America, Inc.

Serban, G. D. (1989). Unwanted inheritance: The psychosocial care of progressive genetic illnesses. *Loss, Grief & Care 3*(3-4), 199-201.

Sherr, L. (1993). HIV testing in pregnancy. In C. Squire (Ed.), *Women and AIDS: Psychological perspectives.* (42-69). Newbury Park, Ca.: Sage.

Silverman, D. C. (1993). Psychosocial impact of HIV-related caregiving on health providers: A review and recommendations for the role of psychiatry. *American Journal of Psychiatry, 150*(5), 705-712.

Squire, C. (Ed.). (1993). *Women and AIDS: Psychological perspectives.* Newbury Park, Ca.: Sage.

Stuber, M. L. (Ed.). (1992). *Children and AIDS.* Washington, D.C.: American Psychiatric Press.

Taylor-Brown, S. & Wiener, L. (1993). Making videotapes of HIV-infected women for their children. *Families in Society: The Journal of Contemporary Human Services, 74*(8), 468-480.

Trice, A. (1988). Posttraumatic stress syndrome-like symptoms among AIDS caregivers. *Psychological Reports, 63,* 656-658.

van der Kolk, B. A. (1987). *Psychological trauma.* Washington D.C.: American Psychiatric Press, Inc.

Wallerstein, R., Seshadri, K., Brady-Yasbin, S., Shih, L., & Wallerstein, D. F. (1994). A retrospective survey of community based utilization of Tay Sachs screening in eight New Jersey counties. *Journal of Genetic Counseling,3,*(2), 125-131.

Wertz, D. C., Fanos, J. H., & Reilly, P. R. (1994). Genetic testing for children and adolescents: Who decides? *Journal of the American Medical Association , 272,*(11), 875-881.

Wiener, L., Theur, S., Steinberg, S. M., Riekert, K. A., & Pizzo, P. A. (1994). The HIV-infected child: Parental responses and psychosocial implications. *American Orthopsychiatric Association, Inc.,* 485-492.

Wiener, L., Moss, H., Davidson, R., & Fair, C. (1992). Pediatrics: The emerging psychosocial challenges of the AIDS epidemic. *Child and Adolescent Social Work Journal, 9*(5), 381-407.

Winnicott, D. W. (1965). *The maturational processes and the facilitating environment.* Connecticut: International Universities Press, Inc.

Worden, J. W. (1982). *Grief counseling and grief therapy: A handbook for the mental health practitioner.* New York: Springer.

Worden, J. W. (1991). Grieving a loss from AIDS. *The Hospice Journal, 7,* 143-150.

Ybarra, S. (1991). Women and AIDS: Implications for counseling. *Journal of Counseling & Development, 69,* 285-287.

Zegans, L. S., Gerhard, A. L., & Coates, T. J. (1994). Psychotherapies for the person with HIV disease. *Psychiatric Clinics of North America, 17*(1), 149-161.

Name Index

Subject Index

Abortion, 21, 22, 32, 73, 91, 92, 102, 107, 112, 117, 119

Acquired Immunodeficiency Syndrome, 12, 14, 15

African-American, 8, 13, 14, 21, 24, 62, 116, 117

AIDS, 3, 4, 5, 6, 7, 8, 11, 12, 13, 14, 15, 16, 17, 18, 19, 20, 21, 22, 24, 25, 26, 29, 30, 32, 33, 34, 41, 45, 46, 51, 52, 53, 58, 62, 63, 65, 66, 67, 73, 74, 75, 77, 79, 81, 82, 83, 84, 85, 86, 87, 88, 89, 90, 91, 93, 94, 95, 96, 97, 98, 99, 100, 101, 102, 103, 105, 106, 107, 108, 109, 110, 112, 113, 114, 115, 116, 117, 118, 119

demographics of, 13

history of, 11

psychological manifestations of, 15, 16, 58, 107

transmission of, 15, 75, 118

AIDS education, 117, 118, 86

AIDS orphans, 8, 110, 108, 118, 119

AIDS-related illnesses, 12, 14, 18, 51, 74, 75, 79, 85, 89, 119

Anger, 23, 25, 26, 27, 42, 45, 47, 58, 59, 79, 89, 93, 97, 56, 94, 108, 110, 112

Anniversary reaction, 79-81

Anticipated death, 6, 8, 25, 32, 45, 46, 61, 63, 78, 81, 82, 91, 93, 94, 95, 97, 98, 99, 100, 102, 108, 110

Anticipatory grief, 23, 25, 59, 60, 79, 97, 106, 107, 110, 115

Antioch New England Graduate School, 67

Anxiety, 28, 42, 44, 54, 56, 59

Assumptive world, 46, 50

Attachment, 6, 7, 8, 21, 24, 25, 28, 29, 34, 39, 41, 42, 43, 44, 45, 48, 60, 63, 73, 83, 85, 87, 90, 91, 92, 93, 94, 95, 97, 98, 99, 100, 102, 105, 106, 108, 110, 111, 115, 117